Walking with Purpose™ Young A

THE OPENING YOUR HEART SERIES

Beloved: *Opening Your Heart, Part I,* is a six-lesson Bible study that lays a strong foundation for our true identity as beloved daughters of God.

Unshaken: *Opening Your Heart, Part II,* is a six-lesson Bible study that fills our spiritual toolbox with exactly what we need to grow stronger in our faith.

Steadfast: *Opening Your Heart, Part III,* a six-lesson Bible study, unpacks why we are hustling for our worth and how to conquer our fears.

THE KEEPING IN BALANCE SERIES
Harmony: Keeping in Balance, Part I
Perspective: Keeping in Balance, Part II
Exhale: Keeping in Balance, Part III

THE DISCOVERING OUR DIGNITY SERIES
Tapestry: Discovering Our Dignity, Part I
Legacy: Discovering our Dignity, Part II
Heritage: Discovering Our Dignity, Part III

For more information on all Walking with Purpose Bible studies please visit us at **walkingwithpurpose.com**

walking with purpose

walking with purpose

Dear Friend,

Welcome to *Steadfast*, part III of the *Opening Your Heart* young adult Bible study series!

This study takes you to the places where the rubber meets the road—the things that can really rob you of joy. We'll look at how to conquer fear, rest in the unknown instead of being paralyzed by confusion, and gain some needed perspective on suffering. It's going to be a good and fruitful journey.

We can gain a lot of insight from excellent journalism, wise friends, and meaty books that lead us to self-discovery. But nothing transforms like Scripture. That's because the Bible is "God-breathed" (2 Tim. 3:16), "living and active" and "able to discern reflections and thoughts of the heart" (Hebrews 4:12). One of the things Scripture can do is cut through our ability to self-deceive. Our hearts are pierced and convicted and we start to see things as they really are instead of just how we want them to be. It also goes to the depths of us with laser-like precision, bringing words of comfort and encouragement to the places that are raw and hurt. **Bible study is not the same as a book study.** So I commend you for taking the time to open your Bible and get into its pages, instead of settling for someone else consuming it and telling you what it's all about. The soul transformation that we are after comes when we do the work of letting God speak directly into our hearts through His Word.

If you had the chance to do the Bible study, *Beloved* (part I in the *Opening Your Heart* series), then you laid a foundation in terms of your true identity, how to have a personal relationship with Jesus, why and how to pray, the difference the Holy Spirit makes, how God the Father is everything you've ever hoped for, and more. The next course in the series, *Unshaken* (Part II in the *Opening Your Heart* series), introduced you to the sacraments and practical tools that can empower you to stay steady in the ups and downs of the spiritual life. *Steadfast* picks up where *Unshaken* left off, helping you to experience genuine transformation, and offering you hope in the places where you have felt defeated. You were never meant to go it alone. Get ready to get to know God more intimately as the *Steadfast* lover of your soul.

My prayer is that you would "Be firm, steadfast, always fully devoted to the work of the Lord, knowing that in the Lord your labor is not in vain." (1 Corinthians 15:58) God sees you, is thrilled with your heart's hunger for Him, and promises that the time you spend to know Him more will not be wasted.

with love and prayers for you~
Lisa Brenninkmeyer
Founder and Chief Purpose Officer, Walking with Purpose

Steadfast
Opening Your Heart Series
Part III

www.walkingwithpurpose.com

Authored by Lisa Brenninkmeyer
Cover and page design by True Cotton
Production management by Christine Welsko

IMPRIMATUR   + William E. Lori, S.T.D., Archbishop of Baltimore

Copyright © 2010–2017 by Walking with Purpose Inc.
All rights reserved. No part of this book may be reproduced in any form by any electronic or mechanical means (including photocopying, recording, or information storage and retrieval) without permission in writing from Walking with Purpose.

Any Internet addresses (websites, blogs, etc.) in this book are offered as a resource, and may change in the future. Please refer to www.walkingwithpurpose.com as the central location for corresponding materials and references.

Printed: January 2018

ISBN: 978-1-943173-13-6

Steadfast: *Opening Your Heart* Series, Part III

TABLE OF CONTENTS

INTRODUCTION

Welcome to Walking with Purpose 3
The Structure of *Opening Your Heart* Series 3
Study Guide Format and Reference Materials 3
Walking with Purpose™ Young Adult Bible Studies 5
Walking with Purpose™ Website 7
Walking with Purpose™ Mission Statement 8
About the Author 8

LESSONS

1 Worthy ~ Owning Your Identity 11
2 Lionhearted ~ Conquering Your Fears 35
3 Unshackled ~ Experiencing Real Transformation 49
4 Valiant ~ Suffering with Purpose 65
5 Welcomed Home ~ Receiving Forgiveness 81
6 Empowered ~ Reading the Bible 95

APPENDICES

1 Saint Thérèse of Lisieux 113

ANSWER KEY 115

PRAYER PAGES 123

Welcome to Walking with Purpose

You have many choices when it comes to how you spend your time—thank you for choosing Walking with Purpose. Studying God's Word with an open and receptive heart will bring spiritual growth and enrichment to all aspects of your life, making every moment that you've invested well worth it.

Each one of us comes to this material from our own unique vantage point. You are welcome as you are. No previous experience is necessary. Some of you will find that the questions in this study cause you to think about concepts that are new to you. Others might find much is a review. God meets each one of us where we are, and He is always faithful, taking us to a deeper, better place spiritually, regardless of where we begin.

The Structure of *Opening Your Heart* Series

The *Opening Your Heart* series is a three-part Bible study, each of which can stand alone, or all three can be completed one after the other. Each six-week Bible study integrates Scripture with the teachings of the Roman Catholic Church to point us to principles that help us manage life's pace and pressure while living with calm and steadiness.

This Bible study can be used on your own, giving you great material for daily Scripture meditation and prayer. It also lends itself well to group discussion. We encourage you to gather your tribe—a handful of friends who want more out of their spiritual lives. The accountability and deeper friendship that will result make it so much easier to live out the truths contained in these pages.

Study Guide Format and Reference Materials

Each of the three parts of *Opening Your Heart* series is divided into three sections:

The first section comprises six lessons, which are divided into five "days" to help you form a habit of reading and reflecting on God's Word regularly. If you are a young woman who has only bits and pieces of time throughout your day to accomplish tasks, you will find this breakdown of the lessons especially helpful. Each day focuses on Scripture readings and related teaching passages, and ends with a Quiet Your Heart reflection, which should lead you to a time of personal prayer. In addition, Day Five includes a Saint's Story; a lesson conclusion; a resolution section, in which you set a goal for yourself based on a theme of the lesson; and short clips from the *Catechism of the Catholic Church*, which are referenced throughout the lesson to complement the Scripture study.

The second section, the appendices, contains supplemental materials referred to during the study.

The third section contains the answer key. You will benefit so much more from the course study if you work through the questions on your own, searching your heart, as this is your very personal journey of faith. The answer key is meant to enhance small group discussion and provide personal guidance or insight when needed.

A memory verse has been chosen for each part of the *Opening Your Heart* series, and we encourage you to memorize each of them as you move through the course. An illustration of the Bible verse can be found at the back of the Bible study, and color versions and phone lock screens can be downloaded from our website.

At the end of the book are pages on which to write weekly prayer intentions.

The Bible
The recommended Bible translations for use in Walking with Purpose studies are: The New American Bible, which is the translation used in the United States for the readings at Mass; The Revised Standard Version, Catholic Edition; and The Jerusalem Bible.

Walking with Purpose™ Young Adult Bible Studies

The *Opening Your Heart* Series

Beloved: *Opening Your Heart, Part I* is a six-lesson Bible study that lays a strong foundation for our true identity as beloved daughters of God. We'll learn that we belong to a family that will never abandon us. We'll encounter grace and practical tools to make God our first priority. Jesus will meet us personally in the pages of His Word, and we'll be transformed as a result.

Unshaken: *Opening Your Heart, Part II* is a six-lesson Bible study that fills our spiritual toolbox with exactly what we need to grow stronger in our faith. We'll discuss why and how we should read the Bible, what difference the sacraments really make in our lives, how to bravely face challenges in our efforts to follow Christ, and the way Mary perfectly mothers us through it all.

Steadfast: *Opening Your Heart, Part III,* a six-lesson Bible study, unpacks why we are hustling for our worth and how to conquer our fears. We'll look at the role of suffering and forgiveness in our lives, and dig deeper into how we can truly change in the areas where we have felt enslaved. We'll explore life purpose, our vocations, and the depth of God's personal love for His beloved children.

The *Keeping in Balance* Series: *Coming Soon*

Harmony: *Keeping in Balance, Part I* is a seven-lesson Bible study that helps us to get a grip on our lives by looking at the importance of authenticity, setting priorities, managing expectations, and having healthy relationships. We'll also explore finding a balance between mediocrity and perfectionism so that we can become the women God created us to be without stressing or striving.

Perspective: *Keeping in Balance, Part II* is a six-lesson Bible study that addresses how we can become more content, grow stronger in areas where we've failed a million times, and get moving when we feel like settling for the status quo. *Perspective* also explores how we can engage our culture as Catholics at a time when the reputation of Christians is at an all-time low.

Exhale: *Keeping in Balance, Part III* is a six-lesson Bible study that helps us establish a rhythm of rest, worship, and surrender. If you long for more simplicity in your life and are ready to order your thoughts so you can experience inner peace, this Bible study will both inspire you and provide you with practical steps to make positive changes.

The *Discovering Our Dignity* Series: *Coming Soon*

Tapestry: *Discovering Our Dignity, Part I* is a six-lesson Bible study that explores the beginning of salvation history through the eyes of the women of Genesis. The difficulties they struggled with are remarkably similar to our own: relationship challenges, the death of dreams, the lure of compromise, and the danger of self-reliance. We'll learn from their mistakes as we apply age-old wisdom to our modern challenges.

Legacy: *Discovering Our Dignity, Part II* is a nine-lesson Bible study that picks up where *Tapestry* left off. Our exploration of the women of salvation history continues as we move further into the Old Testament. We'll explore a myriad of women's issues such as loneliness, shame, leadership challenges, and making a difference in the world.

Heritage: *Discovering Our Dignity, Part III* is a seven-lesson Bible Study that highlights key women of the New Testament. Mary and Martha will help us explore the balance of work and worship, and the poor widow will shed new light on what it means to live sacrificially. We'll be inspired especially by Mary, the Blessed Mother, as we apply her wisdom to our daily challenges.

Walking with Purpose™ Website

Please visit our website at www.walkingwithpurpose.com to find supplemental materials that complement our Bible studies; a link to our online store for additional Bible studies, DVDs, books, and more; and the following free content:

WWP Scripture Printables of our exclusively designed verse cards that complement all Bible studies. Available in various sizes, lock screens for phones, and a format that allows you to e-mail them to friends.

WWP Bible Study Playlists of Lisa's favorite music accompany each Bible study.

WWP Videos of all Connect Coffee Talks by Lisa Brenninkmeyer.

WWP Blog by Lisa Brenninkmeyer, a safe place where you are welcome, where the mask can drop and you can be real. Subscribe for updates.

WWP Leadership Development Program
We are here to help you take your leadership to the next level! Through our training, you'll discover insights that help you achieve your leadership potential. You'll be empowered to step out of your comfort zone and experience the rush of serving God with passion and purpose. We want you to know that you are not alone; we offer you encouragement and the tools you need to reach out to a world that desperately needs to experience the love of God.

Links to WWP Social Media

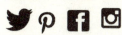

Twitter, Pinterest, Facebook, Instagram

Walking with Purpose™ Mission Statement

Walking with Purpose aims to bring women to a deeper personal relationship with Jesus Christ by offering personal studies and small group discussions that link our everyday challenges and struggles with the solutions given to us through the teachings of Christ and the Roman Catholic Church.

About the Author

Lisa Brenninkmeyer, raised as an evangelical Protestant, entered the Catholic Church in 1991. She has led Bible studies in Europe, Mexico, and the United States, and has written curricula for women and children. She founded Walking with Purpose in 2008 out of a desire to see women come to know Christ personally. Her speaking and writing are inspired by a desire to see women transformed as they realize how much God loves them. She holds a BA in psychology from St. Olaf College. She lives with her husband, Leo, and their seven children in St. Augustine, Florida.

Lessons

NOTES

Walking with Purpose is a community of women growing in faith – together! This is where women are gathering. Join us!

www.walkingwithpurpose.com/find-program-near

Lesson 1

WORTHY ~ OWNING YOUR IDENTITY

Introduction

Her Instagram feed painted a picture of a successful, carefree, full life. Keeping her eye out for "moments" and incorporating white space to give her feed room to breathe made all the difference. If you measured the quality of her days by the beauty depicted on the screen, you'd say she was nailing it. But behind her camera and well-curated public image, she was miserable. She wasn't the only one feeling this way, but few would admit it out loud.

The pressure to hustle for our worth is felt professionally, socially, and even spiritually. At work or school, we want to impress people with our skills, knowledge, intellect, and creativity. We're told that we have to come up with an elevator pitch that communicates all we have to offer—a verbal résumé—and to be ready to share it instantly and winsomely. The concept of personal branding makes us wonder what makes us so special. Deep down, we worry we aren't.

We know we're supposed to have a full social calendar. We wonder if we're filling our time with things we actually enjoy, or if we're just committing to things in order to avoid being alone. The silence of alone time can be scary, because then the questions about our worth, the confusion about what we're doing with our lives, and the insecurities of relationships start to crowd our minds. We want people and activities to distract us from questions that don't seem to have answers.

Our spiritual lives aren't immune to this kind of pressure, either. It's so hard to say, "I am enough. I have done enough." Most of us have some faulty thoughts regarding what kind of a father God is. Lies abound around His love. Even when we've taken time to get to know God personally, the desire to perform for Him in order to earn His love can seep in.

Is there another way to live?

Oh, my friend, there most certainly is. And it is *good*. Freedom can be found if we are willing to let go of habits that keep us shackled. But we'll need to learn to listen to God's voice more intently than we listen to people's opinions. At first, this new way of living might feel awkward. That's an inevitable part of change. But then it will start to feel OK, and ultimately, it will feel like the release and breath of fresh air that we are longing for.

The first step is acknowledging that we have been lied to. Our culture has convinced us to measure our worth by the wrong things. So many of these lies *feel* true, and we have unconsciously embraced them. We need to name them—to bring these false ways of determining our value into the light. Then we need to compare them to what *God* says.

Each day of this lesson, we'll explore one of these destructive lies and compare it to our God-given, true identity. Archbishop Fulton Sheen said, "The truth is the truth even if no one believes it, and a lie is a lie even if everyone believes it." This means that there are some lies that a lot of people believe, and sorting through them all can be confusing. But we are promised in John 8:32 that we *can* know the truth, and *the truth will set us free*.

Day One
THE LIE: MY WORTH IS DETERMINED BY WHAT I LOOK LIKE AND WHAT I DO

THE TRUTH: MY WORTH IS ROOTED IN MY IDENTITY AS A CHERISHED DAUGHTER OF GOD

1. A. List some messages that our culture sends to women in terms of their worth. As you read the list, do any of these messages regularly mess with your mind? If so, which ones?

Worthy ~ Owning Your Identity | 1

B. The author of Psalm 139 had a healthy sense of self-worth. Read Psalm 139:13–15, and record the ways he described himself. Do these words reflect your self-image?

2. A. What do we learn from 1 Samuel 16:7 about the difference between how God sees us and how people measure our worth?

B. What labels have people given you throughout your life? Do you feel boxed in by them? Have you started using these words or labels to describe yourself?

Seeing yourself through the eyes of God doesn't happen automatically. It requires that you be intentional about what you allow to saturate your mind. If this is an area of struggle for you, check where your time goes. Whose voice is getting more airtime in your head—God's words about your worth found in Scripture, or definitions of what is desirable and beautiful found on the Internet?

I find it interesting that the Bible doesn't try to convince us that achievements and appearance don't ever matter. It paints an accurate picture about how the world works, but then draws us toward a mind-set that values God's opinion over man's.

In the book of Esther, the most attractive, alluring, and charming virgins in the country are brought together so the king can try them out and pick a new wife. Their dignity is about to be stripped away, but before they are to be paraded before him, they need to receive beauty treatments—which should cause us to pause and say, "*What?* Weren't these the most beautiful young women in the country?" What was true then is true now. By the world's standards, we'll never be gorgeous enough. There will always be someone prettier and thinner. Beauty is a multibillion-dollar business. Society tells us, "You are only as valuable as you are beautiful," and we are offered product after product to help us become more "valuable."

But our worth isn't measured in the mirror. It's been measured at the cross. And you have already been measured and considered worth *everything* to Jesus. In the words of author and speaker Mark Hart, "You have a God who loves you so much, He would rather die than risk spending eternity without you." His love for you has nothing to do with your outward beauty. It has everything to do with your heart, which is irresistible to Him.

3. A. According to Titus 3:4–5, what had *no bearing* on Jesus' decision to die for us? Which aspects of His character caused Him to make this sacrifice?

   B. How did He save us (Titus 3:5–6)? He saved us so that what would happen (Titus 3:7)?

   C. What state were we in when Jesus saved us? See Romans 5:8.

We're justified by His *grace*—not by our list of accomplishments, personal brand, portfolio, qualifications, or perfection. Jesus decided we were worth dying for and offered us His grace when we were still messed up and falling short of our potential. He invites us to draw near and hear Him whisper, "Beloved," when we are at our worst. No matter what we do or don't do, our worth in His eyes is unchanging. God loves us not because *we* are good, but because *He* is good.

4. A. Because of Jesus, through faith and our baptism, what is our new identity? See Galatians 3:26.

   B. Whom did God send as proof of our adoption as His children? What are we now to call God? See Galatians 4:6.

5. Read Romans 8:14–16 and describe what it means to be adopted children of God.

Quiet your heart and enjoy His presence. . . .

Being led by the Holy Spirit is an indicator that we are daughters of God. Does this mean that whenever we aren't led by the Holy Spirit we stop being God's children? Does our identity falter when we are weak and fail? No. But it does mean that if we are going to act like who we really are, we need to seek guidance from the Holy Spirit, and do what He tells us to do. Being "led by the Spirit" may sound a little ethereal and hard to grasp. We don't need to overcomplicate this. What do you sense that God wants you to do right now? There will always be some areas where we're confused and unsure, but there is usually some clarity around an area where we'd rather do things our own way. Romans 8:14 reminds us that a daughter of God recognizes that she is not her own, that she was purchased for a price on the cross, and that she should go where God is telling her to go. But as a beloved daughter, she trusts that even if it isn't the plan she prefers, it's ultimately for her benefit.

One thing is certain: A daughter of God has no need to fall back into fear. As she grows in trusting God, His love for her, and His consistent delivery on all His promises, fear starts to lose its grip on her heart.

Unlock the fullness of life through gratitude. Take a few minutes to reflect on what it cost Jesus for you to have a new identity as a beloved daughter of God. Thank Him for His unfailing love, described in Jeremiah 31:3: "I have loved you with an everlasting love; I have drawn you with unfailing kindness." Thank Him for loving you more than His own life, and for being unchanging.

Day Two
THE LIE: I NEED A SIGNIFICANT OTHER TO VALIDATE MY WORTH

THE TRUTH: I AM COMPLETE IN CHRIST

1. A. It is the most natural and normal thing in the world to want to be chosen and desired. The alternative—being passed over, dismissed, or rejected—can wound us deeply. Take a moment and look back on your life. When was the first time you experienced disapproval or rejection in a powerful enough way that it led you to question your worth?

   B. What does John 15:16 reveal about how wanted you are?

You are chosen. This truth flies in the face of any sense of inadequacy, all insecurities, and every bit of self-doubt. It delivers the news that no matter who has rejected you, no matter how many times you've received the message that you are not enough, that you are lacking in some way, God chose you, because you are precious to Him. You are wanted. You were made by a God who knows your name, who marked you as His. You belong. You are chosen. Ponder this truth for a moment. Let it sink into your mind and heart, traveling to memories and current places of rejection. Allow His relentless, personal love for you to overpower the self-diminishing thoughts.

Because the truth is, too often we don't take the time to pause and reflect on our true worth and how beloved we are. A painful interaction occurs, the feelings of rejection get shoved down as we try to ignore them, and then we go in search of something or someone to make us feel better. This rarely, if ever, gives us the deep sense of worthiness that we long for.

We really get ourselves into trouble when we expect a man to give us that sense of worth or to fill up what we feel is lacking within us. All too often, we don't know that this is what we are doing. We just have an overwhelming sense that we need a boyfriend or a husband, and that being single is somehow less than being in a relationship.

This actually sets any current or future boyfriend or husband up for failure. There is no way that any person can fill the place in our hearts that is meant for Christ alone. We also are tempted to compromise on qualities that we should look for in someone with whom we are willing to share our hearts.

In Colossians 2:10, we are given an important truth to declare over our lives: *"I am complete in Christ."* This means that He is enough to fill what feels empty. That missing piece of the puzzle of our lives? It's *Him*.

2. What are we challenged to do in Proverbs 4:23?

When you connect deeply with a guy—physically or emotionally—you don't walk away from that relationship unaltered. There's something called "heart glue," and when you separate, you leave a little piece of yourself with that person, and it can really hurt. Maybe you have felt that in your own life.

Proverbs 4:23 calls our heart "the wellspring of life." Another word for *wellspring* is *source*. This means that your heart is the source of your life. If your heart stops beating, you stop living. That's the physical side of it. Emotionally, it's where our feelings dwell.

Our hearts matter to God, and only He can satisfy our longings. Only God will be perfectly tender with our hearts. People in our lives will make mistakes and disappoint at some point. Only God will love us unfailingly with a steadfast, faithful, and merciful love. But He'll never completely satisfy us if we keep looking for someone else to fill us up. He's a gentleman. He won't force His way into our hearts.

3. It's natural to want a person with flesh and bones to comfort and care for us. There's nothing wrong with turning to people with our needs. But it would be such a game changer if we learned to turn to God first. We can't see God, but we can hear His voice. Write out the following verses and underline them in your Bible. These are your love notes from God.

When you feel ugly → Song of Songs 4:7

When you feel alone → Isaiah 41:10

When you feel unlovable → Isaiah 43:4

When you feel insignificant → Isaiah 49:15–16

When you feel afraid → Psalm 34:8

When you need to know someone cares → Psalm 56:9

When you feel angry → Exodus 14:14

When you feel stupid → 1 Corinthians 1:27–29

When you need a hero → John 14:1–3

Worthy ~ Owning Your Identity | 1

Quiet your heart and enjoy His presence. . . . God has a beautiful plan for your life.

Meditate on the following adaptation of the prayer Be Satisfied with Me, by St. Anthony of Padua:

> *Everyone longs to give themselves completely to someone,*
> *To have a deep soul relationship with another,*
> *To be loved thoroughly and exclusively.*
> *But to a Christian, God says, "No, not until you are satisfied,*
> *Fulfilled and content with being loved by Me alone,*
> *With giving yourself totally and unreservedly to Me.*
> *With having an intensely personal and unique relationship with Me alone.*
> *Discovering that only in Me is your satisfaction to be found,*
> *Will you be capable of the perfect human relationship,*
> *That I have planned for you.*
> *You will never be united to another*
> *Until you are united with Me.*
> *Exclusive of anyone or anything else.*
> *Exclusive of any other desires or longings.*
> *I want you to stop planning, to stop wishing, and allow Me to give you*
> *The most thrilling plan existing . . . one you cannot imagine.*
> *I want you to have the best. Please allow Me to bring it to you.*
> *You just keep watching Me, expecting the greatest things.*
> *Keep experiencing the satisfaction that I am.*
> *Keep listening and learning the things that I tell you.*
> *Just wait, that's all. Don't be anxious, don't worry*
> *Don't look around at things others have gotten*
> *Or that I have given them*
> *Don't look around at the things you think you want,*
> *Just keep looking off and away up to Me,*
> *Or you'll miss what I want to show you.*
> *And then, when you're ready, I'll surprise you with a love*
> *Far more wonderful than you could dream of.*
> *You see, until you are ready, and until the one I have for you is ready,*
> *I am working even at this moment*
> *To have both of you ready at the same time.*
> *Until you are both satisfied exclusively with Me*
> *And the life I prepared for you,*
> *You won't be able to experience the love that exemplified your relationship with Me.*
> *And this is perfect love.*
> *And dear one, I want you to have this most wonderful love,*
> *I want you to see in the flesh a picture of your relationship with Me.*
> *And to enjoy materially and concretely the everlasting union of beauty, perfection and love that I*

*offer you with Myself.
Know that I love you utterly. I am God.
Believe it and be satisfied.*"[1]

Day Three
THE LIE: I NEED PEOPLE'S APPROVAL TO BE HAPPY

THE TRUTH: I CAN LIVE FOR AN AUDIENCE OF ONE

This is a lie that does contain some truth, so it's easy to believe. The truth is, it's easier to be happy when people approve of us. But we don't *need* their validation. And if our choices are too influenced by what others think of us, we'll definitely be tempted to compromise.

If we want to grow closer to God, then it's worth pausing to take a look at what motivates our behavior. Ideally, we're motivated by a pure love for God. But in the lives of most women, the opinion of others is a primary motivator. Instead of seeking security and value in God, we look for other people to measure our worth. As a result, our actions are driven by our desire for affirmation, to be noticed, and to be praised: "I'll do, so I can be loved." There is a difference between liking to be appreciated and doing something in order to be appreciated. In the latter case, our value is determined by the opinions of others. We become people-pleasers, motivated more by what those around us want than by what God is calling us to do and be.

The greatest need of a woman who is driven by others' opinions of her is to be loved. Out of a fear of rejection, we define ourselves by how other people perceive us. God calls us to define ourselves by His unconditional love for us. When we settle for the fickle love of other people, it's harder for us to soak up God's love. Ideally, we'll be so filled up with His love that it can spill over into the lives of those around us, helping us to love as Christ loves. But when we're obsessed with what others think of us, we often struggle to have intimate relationships. Our greatest concern is to be affirmed and validated, and so the temptation is enormous to wear a mask and be whoever we think those around us want us to be.

---

[1] "Be Satisfied with Me," The Practicing Catholic, http://thepracticingcatholic.com/2015/06/13/be-satisfied-with-me/ (accessed September 6, 2017).

Oftentimes, when we recognize that we are motivated by others' opinions of us, we find that some of this has come from our relationships with our earthly fathers. If our earthly fathers don't love us unconditionally and communicate that effectively, we will often, as young girls, seek that affirmation from friends. As we get older, we'll seek it from a boyfriend and later, from a husband. In these relationships, we are seeking security. We are seeking affirmation that we are worthy of love. When this is what drives us, we desperately need God's unconditional love to fill us.

1. A. What instructions are we given in 1 Corinthians 16:13?

We have to be on our guard, because our ability to deceive ourselves is sky-high. Unless we're slowing down and asking ourselves hard questions, we'll fail to look at what is motivating our behavior. Paying attention to which people and places tempt us to slip on a mask will help alert us to times when we're probably tempted to compromise who we truly want to be.

We need to stand firm in the faith. As we encounter people whose beliefs differ from ours, we are always to respect where someone else is coming from. At the same time, we need to remain rooted in what we know to be true. If we have tied people's approval to our sense of well-being, it'll be hard to stand firm in the faith. Many followers of Christ feel too Christian for one group and too secular for another. This causes people to feel they don't belong anywhere, which can be pretty unsettling. It requires courage and strength to stand alone.

B. Have you experienced the ache of not belonging? Has the desire to fit in ever tempted you to compromise what you believe? Can you identify any relationships that make it hard for you to courageously stand firm? Share your story here.

2. Poet and activist Maya Angelou wrote, "You are only free when you realize you belong no place—you belong every place—no place at all. The price is high. The reward is great."[2]

I invite you to read that quote again, this time more slowly. At first glance, this might make you think that if she's right, freedom is impossible to achieve. Because who can get rid of the deep desire to belong? What does she mean? How can we belong everyplace and no place at all?

Please hear me on this: I am in no way suggesting that the desire to belong is wrong. I believe it is hardwired within us. The ache to belong is so familiar to me. . . . It makes me think of a memory of all my friends making me walk home from school on the other side of the street because I had danced with the wrong boy during PE in sixth grade. Then countless memories of betrayal by a high school boyfriend whom I had trusted with my heart come to mind, and it still stings. I remember a social event where everything was riding on my winning the approval of the women there. I gave it my best shot, paying attention to my clothes and my facial expressions and my words, but backs literally turned after I was looked up and down with disapproval. After decades of being Catholic I still feel like there is an "inner club" that I will never belong to because I grew up Protestant and am a woman. I have spent decades of my life in pursuit of the holy grail of belonging, and the price I've paid for compromise is too high to count.

Freedom from this way of living . . . oh, this I want. Do you? I think it's worth exploring what Maya Angelou was describing. It has everything to do with learning how to *live for an audience of One*. But even as I read that, I know how easy it would be to think, "OK, so God's opinion is the one that really matters. So I need to perform well for Him." To that, I say an emphatic *no*. We do *not* perform for God.

In trying to flesh out the true meaning of what I'm getting at, a quote from Scottish Olympic athlete and missionary Eric Liddell comes to mind. His words were made famous by the film about his life, *Chariots of Fire*: "God made me fast. And when I run, I feel His pleasure."

How did God make you—your unique personality, passions, and abilities? Which convictions are nonnegotiable for you?

---

[2] Maya Angelou, "A Conversation with Maya Angelou," interview by Bill Moyers, *Bill Moyers Journal*, PBS, November 21, 1973.

As God watches you, it gives Him the most enormous pleasure when you run *your* race, remaining true to who you really are. If you will allow His pleasure to be your deepest motivator, you'll begin to experience a sense of deep belonging when you are being your true self—the woman God created you to be.

3. A. According to Philippians 3:20, where do we belong?

   B. Citizenship denotes membership in a community. How is that community described in Hebrews 12:1?

   C. What is the "great cloud of witnesses" watching us do?

Who are these people described in Hebrews 12:1? They are the great spiritual athletes of the past. It's the communion of saints, the people who have gone before us to heaven and are now cheering us on as we run toward the finish line. It's the people in the Hebrews 11 Hall of Faith: Noah, Abraham, Moses, Rahab, David, Samuel, the apostles . . . all these people who lived through the beatdown of running their race and ended in victory. They are looking at you and saying, "I did it—and so can you! Run your race!"

Hebrews 12 is filled with this imagery of a race being observed. The great cloud of witnesses aren't the only ones there watching. Who else is there as you run? Who is your home team, your tribe? You need at least one person who is there when you fall, who knows how to both commiserate and commission. This is the person who says, "You're right, that really was awful. You really choked. Yeah, it actually was that bad. But you showed up. And that is what matters. That is what counts. You showed courage because that is who you are. You are a courageous warrior— a spiritual athlete—and you are going to get back in the race. I am here to help you to get there." These are the people who really matter, the flesh-and-blood people who are there for you in the low moments and celebrate with you in the high ones. Lean in to these people. Listen to their words. Don't act as if their words don't matter because they already like you. And don't tell them that you are fine when you are not. Lean in. They are one of God's greatest gifts to you.

D. Which person in your life encourages you to show up as your truest self, picks you up when you fall, and speaks words of life to your heart?

Quiet your heart and enjoy His presence. . . . Picture His smile of pleasure as He looks at you, His beloved daughter.

As you run your race, there will always be critics in the arena. You can learn to anticipate their comments and acknowledge their presence, but never make their approval your goal. Look to the great cloud of witnesses for encouragement, and cultivate a "home team" of friends who call out your truest, best self.

But there is One who should have the very best seat in the arena. He has been there Himself and experienced the beatdown of all beatdowns. He gets what it feels like to be shredded and to keep going. The critics? He had hordes of them, and their cruelty surrounded Him when He was at His weakest. His opinion is the one that matters most. In fact, in the end, His is the only one that will count. We are to run with our eyes fixed on Him.

We are to give Him *the best seat in the arena, and never, ever take our eyes off* Him.

It's scary to step out into the arena and embrace the life that we were created to live. It involves training and has a cost. We aren't promised that this marathon will be easy. But we are promised that in the end, we will be face-to-face with the One who has been sitting in the arena all along saying, "Lock your eyes on mine! You can do it! You can walk this path! I went there ahead of you and experienced far worse. And do you know why I did it? So that I could be with you. I did it all for you, for this incredible time when I can welcome you home and bring you into a rest that is like nothing you have ever experienced!"

Fix your eyes on Jesus and become who you were designed to be—the daughter of the King, full of the greatness and glory of your Father. Lift up your head, and run your race.

Day Four
THE LIE: MY SENSE OF WORTH WILL BE HIGHER IF I PUT MYSELF FIRST

THE TRUTH: MY SENSE OF WORTH INCREASES IN PROPORTION TO MY SELF-GIVING

"It's not selfish to do what's best for you."
"Fall in love with taking care of yourself."
"Personal branding got you down? Follow these five easy steps to create clarity and confidence!"
"I'm all about me. My growth, my goals, my happiness, my worth."

For some of us, reading those quotes makes us nod our heads in agreement. We're determined not to be doormats or passed over. Aren't these supposed to be the best years of our lives?

For others, they scream of self-centered, superficial living. Saint Teresa of Calcutta's words come to mind: "A life not lived for others is not a life."

Many of us read these quotes and think they take it a little far, but that self-care has got to factor into the way we live.

Where's the balance? What's the truth?

1. A. What insight do we gain from Jesus in Matthew 6:31–33?

These verses remind me that the problem isn't whether or not my outfit is fashionable. Wearing something ugly or outdated doesn't make me holy, and wearing something cute doesn't make me sinful. What Jesus is pointing out is our tendency to get preoccupied and worried about superficial things. First things first: He asks that our main focus be God's kingdom and our righteousness.

In his book *Making All Things New*, Henri Nouwen puts it this way:

> Jesus does not respond to our worry-filled way of living by saying that we should not be so busy with worldly affairs. He does not try to pull us away

from the many events, activities, and people that make up our lives. He does not tell us that what we do is unimportant, valueless, or useless. Nor does he suggest that we should withdraw from our involvements and live quiet, restful lives removed from the struggles of the world.

Jesus' response to our worry-filled lives is quite different. He asks us to shift the point of gravity, to relocate the center of our attentions, to change our priorities. Jesus wants us to move from the "many things" to the "one necessary thing." It is important for us to realize that Jesus in no way wants us to leave our many-faceted world. Rather, he wants us to live in it, but firmly rooted in the center of all things. Jesus does not speak about a change in activities, a change in contacts or even a change of pace. He speaks about a change of heart. This change of heart makes everything different, even while everything appears to remain the same. This is the meaning of "set your hearts on his kingdom first . . . and all these other things will be given you as well." What counts is where our hearts are. When we worry, we have our hearts in the wrong place.[3]

Take some time to think about Nouwen's words, then read Matthew 6:21. As you reflect on these teachings, where do you think your treasure is? Where is your heart? In other words, what is at the center of your attention?

B. What do you think it means to seek something *first*? What might look different in your life if you rearranged your priorities regarding your time and put God's kingdom and your righteousness first?

One practical way to look at the word *first* is to think about the way we start the day.

What do we grab first? The phone or the Bible?

Whom do we talk to first? Our friend or God?

---

[3] Henri Nouwen, *Making All Things New* (New York: HarperCollins, 1981), 17.

Where do we look for the day's schedule first? The calendar or the guidance of the Holy Spirit?

I'm not suggesting that we ignore a schedule or never make a to-do list. But I do think it helps us set our priorities when we look at our calendars *while* talking to the Lord, letting Him know that these events and commitments are what we think matter most, but that we recognize He may have a different plan. Starting the day with this attitude can help us view inevitable interruptions as divine appointments.

2. What insights do you gain from the following New Testament verses about a life of self-sacrifice?

   Matthew 6:24–25

   John 12:24–25

   Philippians 3:8

3. Sometimes what discourages us from a life of self-giving is a feeling that the little we can do doesn't make much of a difference. If it isn't Instagram-worthy, we can be tempted to think it doesn't matter. It's also easy to be overwhelmed by the tremendous needs around us. We might think to ourselves, "I'm not Mother Teresa. I can't begin to address the major things that are wrong in the world." All too often, because we can't do something great, we just binge-watch Netflix.

   If our saint of Calcutta were sitting with us, I wonder how she'd respond. Let's let her speak for herself. Read the following quotes by Mother Teresa, and journal your thoughts. Does one quote stand out to you? Do you feel convicted? Motivated?

   "We know only too well that what we are doing is nothing more than a drop in the ocean. But if the drop were not there, the ocean would be missing something."[4]

   "Do not think that love in order to be genuine has to be extraordinary. What we need is to love without getting tired. Be faithful in small things because it is in them that your strength lies."[5]

---

[4] "Quotes About Ocean," Goodreads, https://www.goodreads.com/quotes/tag/ocean (accessed September 27, 2017).

"In this life we cannot do great things. We can only do small things with great love."[6]

"At the end of life we will not be judged by how many diplomas we have received, how much money we have made, how many great things we have done. We will be judged by 'I was hungry, and you gave me something to eat, I was naked and you clothed me. I was homeless, and you took me in.'"[7]

"Do not wait for leaders; do it alone, person to person."[8]

"If you are humble nothing will touch you, neither praise nor disgrace, because you know what you are."[9]

A. My thoughts:

B. If you could help one group of people in the world, whom would it be and what would you do?

Quiet your heart and enjoy His presence. . . . You cannot outgive God.

Hardwired into each of our souls are "longings for the infinite and for happiness" (CCC 33). According to the Catechism, this "desire [for happiness] is of divine origin: God has placed it in the human heart in order to draw man to the One who alone can fulfill it: We all want to live happily; in the whole human race there is no one who does not assent to this proposition, even before it is fully articulated" (CCC 1718).

This is a good, holy, and God-given desire. But we get ourselves in trouble when we seek to have that desire satisfied in superficial ways. Unfortunately, sometimes we gain just enough pleasure that we

---

[5] "Mother Teresa Quote," Great-Quotes.com, http://www.great-quotes.com/quote/141903 (accessed September 27, 2017).

[6] Quotationsbook, http://quotationsbook.com/quote/24701/ (accessed September 27, 2017).

[7] Goodreads, https://www.goodreads.com/quotes/759-at-the-end-of-life-we-will-not-be-judged (accessed September 27, 2017).

[8] Goodreads, https://www.goodreads.com/quotes/12081-do-not-wait-for-leaders-do-it-alone-person-to (accessed September 27, 2017).

[9] Goodreads, https://www.goodreads.com/quotes/55677-if-you-are-humble-nothing-will-touch-you-neither-praise (accessed September 27, 2017).

stop seeking deeper fulfillment and satisfaction. Our focus turns inward, and our perspective can quickly grow dark and hopeless. It's as our focus turns outward that light rushes into our souls, filling us with the perspective we need to remain grateful at all times and suffer well when that is required.

When we make our self-worth the highest good or our main focus, we will not experience the fullness of life we were created for. The abundant life is found in self-giving.

In the words of Saint John Paul II:

> *It is Jesus that you seek when you dream of happiness; He is waiting for you when nothing else you find satisfies you; He is the beauty to which you are so attracted; it is He who provoked you with that thirst for fullness that will not let you settle for compromise; it is He who urges you to shed the masks of a false life; it is He who reads in your heart your most genuine choices, the choices that others try to stifle.*
>
> *It is Jesus who stirs in you the desire to do something great with your lives, the will to follow an ideal, the refusal to allow yourselves to be ground down by mediocrity, the courage to commit yourselves humbly and patiently to improving yourselves and society, making the world more human and more fraternal.*[10]

Take a few moments to quiet down and listen for the Holy Spirit's guidance. Is He asking you to shed a mask? To let go of some things that are preoccupying you and taking up too much of your time? Do you need to ask the Lord for courage to overcome some fears? Talk to Him about His plans for your life. His plans are for your good—to prosper and not to harm you, to give you a future full of hope (Jeremiah 29:11). Offer Him your best, your all. You will not be disappointed.

"Perhaps you were born for such a time as this." (Esther 4:14)

Day Five
SAINT'S STORY

Saint Catherine of Siena

How did an uneducated woman in the Middle Ages grow to be so influential that Pope Gregory XI not only listened to her, but did what she said? This powerful

---

[10] Goodreads, https://www.goodreads.com/author/quotes/6473881.Pope_John_Paul_II (accessed September 26, 2017).

figure, Saint Catherine of Siena, was truly remarkable and intriguing. She was born in 1347 in Siena, Italy, and from childhood, she had visions of Christ and an unusual intimacy with Him, the Virgin Mary, and the saints in heaven. A true mystic, Saint Catherine lived in the realm of the spiritual, connecting heaven and earth in her day-to-day life. Although she never studied theology, she is a Doctor of the Church, meaning her teachings are for the whole Church. She's considered a teacher for the ages.

Her life of extreme asceticism (she was so committed to fasting that she hardly ate anything) and her otherworldly visions might make you believe that people thought she was crazy. When she prayed, she entered a state of such ecstasy that she was totally unresponsive to anyone or anything around her, not even wincing when a needle was put in her hand. But the people who were honored and respected during the medieval period were of a different sort than the individuals we honor in our culture. The most respected men and women were those who were in touch with the sacred. Most important, Saint Catherine's life was so exemplary—sacrificial, pious, and devout—that her good character and overall wisdom made it impossible to consider her insane. Her life was looked at in its entirety, and she shone among all others as a standout—a leader, a witness, a saint. Caring for the sick (especially during the black plague) and going where no one else wanted to serve revealed her self-forgetful love for all.

Saint Catherine of Siena lived during a time when the pope was living in Avignon, France, instead of Rome. The Church was falling into financial and moral ruin, and Saint Catherine believed that the key to its survival was for the pope to return to Rome. So at age twenty-eight, she traveled to Avignon, got an audience with the pope (her reputation preceded her), and convinced him to return to the Eternal City. She remained committed to Pope Gregory and his successor in Rome, Pope Urban VI, until her death.

Quotes and teachings of Saint Catherine of Siena continue to inspire us today, regardless of how many years ago they were spoken. Our hearts are stirred when we read her words, "Be who God meant you to be and you will set the world on fire." She believed this wholeheartedly, and knew that our ability to live this radically and impact the world so significantly would require a high level of self-forgetfulness. Our obsession with putting our best face forward on social media is quite a contrast to the kind of living she recommended. "What is it you want to change?" Saint Catherine asked. "Your hair, your face, your body? Why? For God is in love with all those things and he might weep when they are gone."[11] To Saint Catherine of Siena, all that

---

[11] AZ Quotes, http://www.azquotes.com/author/17881-St_Catherine_of_Siena, (accessed October 20, 2017).

mattered was what her Beloved thought of her. His love was intoxicating, consuming, and more than enough to deeply satisfy her.

Saint Catherine of Siena suffered, as all the saints have. Instead of running from it, she welcomed it as an opportunity to strip away self-preoccupation and focus her mind and heart fully on Jesus. Her union with Jesus was worth everything. She truly experienced a mystical marriage with Christ. Before you write this off as an experience reserved for the spiritual giants, I assure you, it isn't something set aside only for the saints. Jesus took on human flesh and came to us all seeking intimacy. This is what He desires with you and me. In Saint Catherine's words, "We are of such value to God that He came to live among us . . . and to guide us home. He will go to any length to seek us, even to being lifted high upon the cross to draw us back to Himself. We can only respond by loving God for His love."[12]

In Matthew 10:39, Jesus says, "Whoever finds his life will lose it, and whoever loses his life for my sake will find it." Saint Catherine of Siena lost herself in Christ, and in doing so, she found the deepest fulfillment, intimacy, belonging, and joy. Her abandonment to God's will allowed her to trust Him utterly and say, "He will provide the way and the means, such as you could never have imagined. Leave it all to Him, let go of yourself, lose yourself on the cross, and you will find yourself entirely."[13]

What can we do to keep a balance between healthy self-care and self-centeredness? In what way would you like to grow in self-forgetfulness?

Conclusion

We long for concrete purpose and direction in life. The last thing we want is to feel we are floating around with no vision for the future. Living in the land of "what if's" can be incredibly unsettling, and we feel so much more *worthy* when we know we are doing what God made us to do. This desire to discover our vocations is normal and good. But before we can discern our vocation– our mission in life– we need to be rooted in our true identity as daughters of God. This must come first or we'll run the risk of living as human *doings* instead of human *beings*. When we discover our true worth as unconditionally loved daughters, we can rest in the reality that nothing we do can earn more or less of God's love.

---

[12] Ibid.
[13] Ibid.

The Catholic Church teaches that there are three primary vocations: married life, the priesthood, and consecrated life. All of these vocations are related to our roles in life and our callings. Our secondary vocation is the unique way in which we use our God-given gifts and talents to help others.

Discovering our primary and secondary vocations requires discernment and patience. If we are going to live intentionally, we should put in the time to identify our specific callings, but we need to be careful that we never allow our work or ministry to define us. When we lose ourselves in a role or a calling and connect our performance to our identity, we'll forfeit the steadiness and confidence that is our birthright as daughters of God. God's approval is the only one that matters. He is calling us to step out into a broken world with giving hearts, not counting numbers or comparing size of mission, but simply showing up and loving sacrificially.

Perhaps you know exactly what God has called you to, exactly where He wants you to be serving. If your vocation is clear, know that you are truly fortunate. Most young women (and older ones as well, actually) aren't sure exactly what they are being called to do. It isn't a matter of not wanting to make a difference or being unwilling to serve. There's just a lack of clarity regarding the where and the what.

Do you know that when God created you, He also created a specific work that you are expected to do? There are certain tasks with your name on them that God wants you to accomplish. Ephesians 2:10 says that "we are God's handiwork, created in Christ Jesus to do good works, that God prepared in advance for us to do."

The key is identifying what those good works are. God has planted seeds in your soul—seeds of discontent. When you see something in the world that you just can't stand, that may be one of the things He wants you to do something about. Truly, miracles happen when a young woman says, "I just can't stand this anymore," and turns to God for guidance. When you feel anger, righteous indignation, frustration, and compassion welling up in you, turn to God and ask Him, "Is this it? Is this one of the things that you created me to do something about?" At some point in your life, you will find that one thing, that stirring of passion that God has placed in your heart.

There are a myriad of things that aren't right around us, but what is the one issue, the one group of people, the one thing that really gets you worked up? It doesn't matter if it's something you figure is too big for you to solve. What is it that grabs your heart? That breaks your heart? That gets you up off the couch saying, "Something has got to be done about that"?

Perhaps it is something connected to an experience of suffering in your life. Please know that none of your tears of pain will be wasted by God. He can use every ounce of what you have been through to make this world a better place. In 1 Corinthians 1:4 we are taught that God "encourages us in our every affliction, so that we may be able to encourage those who are in any affliction with the encouragement with which we ourselves are encouraged by God."

Whatever heartache you have been through has uniquely equipped you to step out and minister to people going through the same thing. There is such a difference between someone saying, "I'm sorry," and someone saying, "I understand, because I've been there." Past trauma shouldn't define us, but it can equip us for life-changing ministry and impact.

In his book *Holy Discontent*, Bill Hybels writes: "I assure you, there is a holy discontent with your name on it. There is something out there that God is waiting for you to grab on to so that he can use you to help solve it. It wrecks you, it wrecks him and he's ready for you *both* to do something about it."[14]

Together, you can set the world on fire.

My Resolution

"My Resolution" is your opportunity to write down one specific, personal application from this lesson. We can take in a lot of information from studying the Bible, but if we don't translate it into action, we have totally missed the point. In James 1:22, we're told that we shouldn't just hear the Word of God; we are to "do what it says." So what qualities should be found in a good resolution? It should be **personal** (use the pronouns *I, me, my, mine*), it should be **possible** (don't choose something so far-fetched that you'll just become discouraged), it should be **measurable** (a specific goal to achieve within a specific time period), and it should be **action oriented** (not just a spiritual thought).

Examples:

1. I struggle to see myself the way God sees me. To help renew my mind, I will memorize 1 Samuel 16:7 ("God does not see as a mortal, who sees the appearance. The LORD looks into the heart.") or Song of Songs 4:7 ("You are beautiful in every way, my friend, there is no flaw in you."), so the Holy Spirit can bring this verse to my mind when I am feeling bad about myself.

---

[14] Bill Hybels, *Holy Discontent* (Grand Rapids, MI: Zondervan, 2007), 54.

2. I feel like I wear a mask with so many of my friends. I will either determine to be real with a carefully chosen few, or find a new friend whom I can trust with my heart. Either way, I will step out of my comfort zone and take a risk to be real.

3. I will go to adoration and ask God to help me take a look at times in my life when I have suffered. I will ask Him if there is someone He wants me to reach out to so that I can offer comfort as someone who has "been there." Then I will follow through, reaching out to that person with a phone call, text, or an offer to get together.

My resolution:

Catechism Clips

CCC 33 The *human person*: with his openness to truth and beauty, his sense of moral goodness, his freedom and the voice of his conscience, with his longings for the infinite and for happiness, man questions himself about God's existence. In all this he discerns signs of his spiritual soul. The soul, the "seed of eternity we bear in ourselves, irreducible to the merely material," can have its origin only in God.

CCC 1718 The Beatitudes respond to the natural desire for happiness. This desire is of divine origin: God has placed it in the human heart in order to draw man to the One who alone can fulfill it:

> We all want to live happily; in the whole human race there is no one who does not assent to this proposition, even before it is fully articulated.

> How is it, then, that I seek you, Lord? Since in seeking you, my God, I seek a happy life, let me seek you so that my soul may live, for my body draws life from my soul and my soul draws life from you.

> God alone satisfies.

Lesson 2

LIONHEARTED ~ CONQUERING YOUR FEARS

Introduction

The storms of the rainy season in Guadalajara, Mexico, were powerful and breathtakingly intense. The kids loved it when we'd take our Suburban out in the midst of a storm. They'd scream with excitement as the water broke over the hood of the car and splashed on their windows, climbing up the sides of the car. Smaller cars would start to float around the roads, out of control. The sensible thing would have been to stay home, but we loved the thrill of being out in the middle of it all, and we had (somewhat groundless) confidence in our Suburban's ability to stay steady no matter what. Our kids liked the rain and the sense of adventure that the storms would bring.

At least that was the case until one particularly crazy storm. We were all at home, enjoying the afternoon, when the rains began. Five-year-old Amy was playing in her bedroom and I was reading in the living room. Bedrooms were on one side of the house, the kitchen on the other, and the two-story, open living room was in the middle with skylights covering most of the ceiling. The rain started calmly enough, but all of a sudden, noises began to explode as hail pelted the skylights. There was a crack, and as I looked up to see the skylights shattering and raining down shards of glass everywhere, Amy appeared at the doorway of her bedroom. Terrified, she began to run through the flying glass to get to me.

And I froze.

I froze. What kind of a mother *freezes* at a time like that? The same mother who knows the Heimlich maneuver yet froze when her three-year-old was choking on a marble. Thank heavens someone with a cool head was nearby to help. I don't know why on earth that has been my reaction not once, but twice, and thank the Lord our brave babysitter was in the kitchen and ran through the glass to rescue Amy. But fear can do that. It can be utterly paralyzing at the absolute worst times imaginable.

Not surprisingly, Amy wasn't so fond of rain after that. And like clockwork, we could count on a daily storm during the rainy season. My response was to comfort her and hold her, to play music loudly during the storms to drown out the sound of the rain. Her daddy's approach was a little different. When the storm would start, he would scoop her up and take her outside. He'd ask her to look at his face, and then he'd smile and talk about how much he loved the rain. He'd stomp in the puddles and make it all a game. Little by little, as she'd watch his lack of fear and total comfort in the storm, she got to the point where she would stomp in the puddles herself. Fear didn't get the last word.

Jesus desires that peace rule in each of our hearts. Yet many people live paralyzed by fear. Panic attacks are on the rise; in any given year, about one-third of American adults have at least one. Sometimes one can see the effects of fear in people in the form of phobias or fearful behavior. But more often, we hide our fears in our hearts. Sometimes even our best friends don't know our secret fears, but they are there, robbing us of the joy that Jesus wants each of us to experience every day. During this lesson, we'll explore ways we can conquer our fears, allowing them to come under the control of God's loving hand.

Day One
AFRAID OF THE STORM

The emotion of fear is a gift insofar as it alerts us to danger. Our senses become heightened, and we look for a way out. Fear lets us know the storm is coming or has hit, but it's not enough to get us *through* the storm. We need something more than that.

Read Matthew 14:22–33.

1. What shift in focus caused Peter to start sinking in the waves? How was he saved from drowning?

2. What kind of a spirit has God given us? See 2 Timothy 1:7.

A spirit of fear will alert us to danger and sharpen our senses, but it will never provide us with what we need to navigate the storms of life. To make it through those circumstances, we need supernatural power, God's unconditional love, and the self-control that helps us choose to dwell on certain things and not others. The good news is, this is exactly what the indwelling Holy Spirit provides. If we replace our spirit of fear with the Spirit of power, love, and self-control, we can conquer our fears.

3. In what ways have you seen God's power in your life? When have you experienced His unconditional love? Has He ever strengthened you by helping you to have self-control in an area of weakness? Share your experiences here and let God's track record of faithfulness increase your confidence in Him. Whatever you face, His presence within you will make all the difference.

Quiet your heart and enjoy His presence. . . . Allow God to dispel your fear.

Fear is unavoidable, but what we choose to do with it is up to us. In the very moment that we feel afraid, we can remind ourselves, "God has not given us a spirit of cowardice but rather of power and love and self-control" (2 Timothy 1:7). That is what is inside us.

When panic hits, grab hold of Jesus' hand. Lock your eyes on the truth that you are not alone, that He is present, and that His presence makes all the difference. Ask Him to dispel your fear.

"You who dwell in the shelter of the Most High, who abide in the shade of the Almighty, say to the Lord, 'My refuge and fortress, my God in whom I trust.'" (Psalm 91:1–2)

"I learned that courage was not the absence of fear but the triumph over it. The brave man is not he that doesn't feel afraid, but he who conquers that fear." —Nelson Mandela

Opening Your Heart Series, Part III

Day Two
AFRAID OF WALKING ALONE AT NIGHT

A survey conducted by Chapman University, in California, discovered that one of Americans' greatest fears is walking alone at night.[15] When people answered the survey, they were probably thinking of the dark alley, the dimly lit parking lot—that sort of thing. I understand this fear. Once the sun goes down, I imagine someone is hiding under my car in the mall parking lot, just waiting to slash my ankles. I start to regret that my hair is always in a ponytail because that's easy for some ne'er-do-well to grab. I walk with my finger over the alarm button on my key fob because you just never know. So I get being freaked out at night.

Night can mean all that—or it can be a metaphor for a general darkness in our circumstances or a darkness in our souls. And we are very afraid of walking through those times alone. That's when walking with your hair down and the key fob in hand just doesn't offer much comfort. So what does Scripture have to say to that fear? Let's dive in. There are lots of verses to look up today, friends. But hang with me. You might end up discovering a couple that you'll carry with you from now on.

1. Did Jesus promise that if we follow Him, He'll remove all challenges from our lives? See John 16:33.

2. What did Saint Teresa of Ávila learn from her experience of trusting God in every circumstance? See CCC 227.

3. Look up the following verses. What does each teach you about walking through darkness?

   A. Deuteronomy 31:6

---

[15] Jolie Lee, "Biggest American Fear? Walking Alone at Night, Survey Finds," *USA Today*, October 22, 2014, http://www.usatoday.com/story/news/nation-now/2014/10/22/fear-study-chapman-university/17663861/.

B. Psalm 27:1 and John 8:12

C. Isaiah 41:10

D. Romans 8:28

4. Which of these verses helps you the most in dealing with your fears? Write it down on an index card and carry it with you.

Quiet your heart and enjoy His presence. . . . God does His finest work in the darkness.

"God has to work in the soul in secret and in darkness because if we fully knew what was happening and what Mystery, transformation, God and Grace will eventually ask of us, we would either try to take charge or stop the whole process." —Saint John of the Cross

The deepest soul work is done in the darkness, and it isn't a group exercise. There are times when God allows us to go to places that we wouldn't choose to go, because it is only there that we will be transformed in the most beautiful of ways. But we shouldn't be afraid of this, because God accompanies us there. We never walk in darkness alone. True, we may feel alone. But our feelings don't define reality. God does. And He promises never to leave us. He is there in the secret places in a way that our minds don't really comprehend.

Take the verse you chose for question 4 and personalize it. Turn it into a prayer of thanksgiving. For example, using Isaiah 41:10, you could pray:

Dear Lord,

Thank you for making it so that I do not need to be afraid, because you are with me. I don't need to be anxious, because you are my God. Thank you for strengthening me. Thank you for helping me. Thank you for upholding me with your victorious right hand. Thank you for grasping hold of me and never letting me go.

Day Three
AFRAID OF REJECTION

We don't always recognize this as a personal struggle because we don't connect the fear of rejection with its fruits. This fear manifests itself as people-pleasing, approval seeking, a heightened sensitivity to criticism, feelings of worthlessness, and a rejection of others so that we turn away before they do. We need to get to the root of this fear if we want to walk in freedom.

1. How does Proverbs 29:25 describe "fear of man" or "fear of others"? Note: The phrase used in the Bible to describe being a people-pleaser or caring too much what others think of us is "fear of man."

A snare is a trap that typically has a noose of wire or a cord. Caring too much what others think is a snare that strangles our freedom. It causes us to crave approval and fear rejection, and puts people in a place meant for God alone.

2. We all experience rejection at some point in our lives. It's unavoidable. But being afraid of it or totally train wrecked by it is actually optional. It all boils down to what our identity is based on. If our worth is defined through people's acceptance of us, then fear of rejection will always be a noose around our necks. But if we can totally embrace the truth that **people's opinions do not determine our worth or identity, that our worth is determined by God and our identity is rooted in being His beloved daughter**, then freedom can be ours.

God's approval is the only one that ultimately matters, and He *adores you*. Yes, *you*. You are not an exception to the rule, no matter what you've done or what you're struggling with today.

What insight do the following verses give as we seek to please God and find our identity in Him?

Romans 8:31

Galatians 1:10

Colossians 3:23

3. Do you struggle with a fear of rejection? If so, in what specific way? (Typical manifestations of this fear are people-pleasing, approval seeking, sensitivity to criticism, feelings of worthlessness, tendency to reject others.)

Quiet your heart and enjoy His presence. . . . Do you want God to show up in your life in a powerful way? Are you tired of the status quo and ready for more? Would you like to see God, in all His glory, intersect your circumstances?

God wants us to experience His glory. He wants to pour out His power on us and to see us living freed, transformed lives. This has always been His desire. When Jesus walked the earth, there was nothing He wanted more—for the people to see His glory and to be changed as a result. But so many of them missed it. Why? The reason is found in the Gospel of John: "For they preferred human praise to the glory of God" (John 12:43). They wanted something more than God's power and glory. They wanted human praise.

Jesus is turning to you now and asking, "What do you want?" How will you answer Him?

Day Four
AFRAID TO LEAN IN TO JOY

"What if I fall?
Oh, my darling, what if you fly?"[16]

1. Jesus came to set us free from the fears that hold us back from soaring as God's beloved daughters. How is the life He desires for us described in the following verses?

    John 10:10

---

[16] Erin Hanson, "Just My Poems," The Poetic Underground,
http://thepoeticunderground.com/post/87639964775/the-talent-of-all-of-you-astounds-me-this-a-quote.

1 Timothy 6:17 (the second part of the verse)

Isaiah 30:18

These verses paint a picture of God wanting us to live deeply satisfying, meaningful, joy-filled lives. These are God's own words, so we can count on them as truth.

But how often do we believe the lies instead? All too often, we don't see God as a gracious, generous father. We believe the lie that He's going to hold out on us (this, of course, was the thought that got things spiraling out of control in the Garden of Eden). Some of us believe the lie that God is a disinterested father. Disaster might be just around the corner, but He's too busy with other things to do anything about it.

Believing lies about God really messes with our ability to embrace and live the life we were created for.

Have you ever realized that your life is going pretty well, and instead of resting in the joy of that moment and thanking God for all He's given, you think, "Oh, no! The other shoe is about to drop"? In her vulnerability research, Dr. Brené Brown has found that the most terrifying, difficult emotion we experience is *joy*. We're afraid to lean in to joy, because the thought of it being taken away is so scary. She describes our mental response as "dress-rehearsing tragedy":

> Dress rehearsing tragedy, she explains, is imagining something bad is going to happen when in reality, nothing is wrong. "How many of you have ever . . . [woken] up in the morning and thought, 'Oh my gosh, job's going great. Parents are good. This can't last.'"[17]

This isn't how God wants us to live. He wants us to lean in to joy and soar! So how do we do that? How can we break free of our tendency to pull back in fear and miss our lives because we are living in the gray?

---

[17] "Brené Brown: 'Joy Is the Most Vulnerable Emotion We Can Experience,'" *Huffington Post*, October 27, 2013, http://www.huffingtonpost.com/2013/10/18/brene-brown-joy-numbing-oprah_n_4116520.html.

2. Hidden in the meaning of the word *Eucharist* is one of the ways we can lean in to the joy we were created for. *Eucharist* means "thanksgiving." Practicing gratitude is one of the best ways to live a life of joy.

   List an area of your life where you fear something that is currently wonderful going awry. What are you afraid of specifically?

   Practice gratitude by listing all the things you are grateful for about that very area of your life.

It's up to you. You decide which of those lists you are going to dwell on. One will leave you paralyzed by the fear of "what if." The other will lead you to joy.

3. Underneath our reluctance to really embrace joy is the fear that we will fall. And consciously or not, we figure that the higher the place we're falling from, the more it will hurt. So we climb down from the peak of joy and sit in the middle ground of low expectations because it feels safer. And life passes us by.

   I can't promise you that you will never fall or that life will never bring you pain. But God makes us promises in Scripture that should make an enormous difference in the way we live. In Deuteronomy 33:27, He promises, "The eternal God is your refuge, and underneath are the everlasting arms." Write that verse below. Think about it. Why does this truth matter? What difference does it make to you personally?

Quiet your heart and enjoy His presence. . . . The Lord is your refuge.

Have you whispered these questions?

"What if I fall?"
"What if I fall because of disappointment?"
"What if I fall because of tragedy?"
"What if I fall because I'm just not good enough?"

Lean in and listen, my friend. If you fall, God will catch you. It's as simple as that. He promises that underneath you, no matter what height you are falling from, His everlasting arms are there to catch you. What do we find at the end of our resources, the end of our dreams, the end of our hopes? We find God's mercy. We find God's graciousness. We find shelter from the storm.

That shelter is available to you right now. "He will shelter you with his pinions, and under his wings you may take refuge" (Psalm 91:4). Come under His wings in prayer. Rest in safety.

"Because he clings to me I will deliver him; because he knows my name I will set him on high. He will call upon me and I will answer, I will be with him in distress; I will deliver him and give him honor. With length of days I will satisfy him, and fill him with my saving power." (Psalm 91:14–16)

Rest in these promises.

Don't miss your life.

Day Five
SAINT'S STORY

Blessed Anne of Saint Bartholomew, Saint Frances Xavier Cabrini, and Saint Joan of Arc

What God is asking of us—to cast our fears aside and follow Him, and to become saints and bring His message of hope to everyone around us through word, deed, and example—is too much for us. The funny thing is that He knows we can't do this without His help. He said it a long time ago: "I am the vine, you are the branches. Whoever remains in me, with me in him, bears fruit in plenty; for *cut off from me you can do nothing*" (John 15:5). When we experience fear in our pursuit of God's purpose for our life, it's because we are forgetting about that. Almost always, our fears are the result of depending too much on ourselves and not trusting enough in God, who is so powerful that He can turn even the most bitter failures (Christ's death on the cross) into the most glorious victories (Easter Sunday). Jesus put it concisely: "For men, it is impossible, but not for God, because everything is possible for God." The more we think about God's omnipotence and love, the more we fill our imagination with His goodness and the wonders He has done in so many lives throughout history, the more easily we will be able to overcome our fears and undertake the Christian adventure in which "the Spirit comes to the aid of our weakness" (Romans 8:26).

This was an especially difficult lesson for Blessed Anne of Saint Bartholomew. She came from a poor shepherding family in sixteenth-century Spain. As a Carmelite nun, Blessed Anne was sent to Belgium and France to start Carmelite convents, and to be prioress in some of them. She would often complain to our Lord that she was too ignorant and shy to be given such important responsibilities. In fact, she complained so much that finally He had to appear to her to calm her down. She had just tried to convince Him that He should choose someone else to do the work she was being asked to do, someone more intelligent, better educated, and more outgoing. So our Lord appeared to her and said, "It is with straw that I start my fires." He didn't comfort her by telling her how great she was. He simply wanted to do things in and through her, if she would let Him.

Saint Frances Xavier Cabrini, America's first canonized saint, illustrates this truth in a more down-to-earth way. She was born in Northern Italy in the 1800s. Early on, she experienced a strong desire to become a missionary, but no religious order would accept her because she had unstable health. So she gathered a group of companions and started her own religious order under the protection of her bishop. Soon she received approval from the pope and began her tireless apostolate with the poor Italian immigrants throughout the Americas. Her work required extensive travel between Europe and America. She ended up crossing the Atlantic more than thirty times on those clunky, uncomfortable, old-fashioned ocean liners. To do so, she had to overcome a mortal fear of water that she acquired after falling into a river and almost drowning when she was just a girl. That fear never left her; God never took it away. Even after years of sea travel, she declined an invitation from her sisters to go for a leisurely boat ride one day because she was afraid of the water! She told them, "I admit my weakness: I am afraid of the sea, and if there is no very holy motive in view, I have no courage to go where I fear danger."

Perhaps the most remarkable example of how trusting in God enables us to overcome fear is found in the truly amazing person of Saint Joan of Arc. A teenage girl, illiterate, of peasant stock, unable to ride horses, and unschooled in war, she received a call from God to liberate a divided and corrupt France from the overpowering and almost complete English invasion toward the end of the Hundred Years' War in the 1300s. No wonder she at first resisted the imprecations of the voices she heard (i.e. the saints whom God sent to her as His messengers)! They continually brought her God's message for four years before she finally obeyed when she was eighteen years old. It was only when they told her, "It is God who commands it," that she complied, entrusting herself completely to God's power. And the world has never been the same. She led armies, outfoxed evil courtiers, emboldened a cowardly king, revived an entire nation, and befuddled the most learned clerics and lawyers of her day. This illiterate teenager single-handedly reversed the fortunes of France and altered the history of Europe while enduring moral, physical, and psychological tortures of the cruelest kind. Through it all, she suffered profoundly, including confusion, exhaustion, and betrayal, ultimately being burned at the stake, dying with Jesus' name on her virgin lips.

And why? "It is God who commands it." She was able to do it because she *hoped in God*. She knew that serving God was her only true occupation, and that He would always be faithful to those who serve Him truly. Saint Joan of Arc left us a message: "Hope in God. Put your trust in Him, and He will deliver you from your enemies [fears]." Indeed, only God will never disappoint us; only He is worthy of our unbridled hope. When we feel helpless or fearful of all that Christ is asking of us, that's what we need to remember.

What fears are you facing in your life right now? How can Blessed Anne, Saint Frances, and Saint Joan of Arc inspire you to deal with them?

Conclusion

There hasn't been a moment of my life when I welcomed or sought out suffering. What I often forget is that it may be the very thing I need to experience in order to become the woman God wants me to be. Whenever I begin to think, "Surely, I shouldn't have to suffer since I try to do the right thing and live the way God wants me to," I think of the cross. It seems like the worst thing that could happen to anyone—defeat, humiliation, pain—but it was the ultimate victory and the accomplishment of our salvation.

So how do I conquer my fears? It's a journey. Sometimes it feels like two steps forward and one step back. But even then, progress is being made.

Because I'm so prone to fall back into fear, I frequently have to remind myself of the lessons contained in the points that follow. When fear starts to get the better of me, I go back to these lessons to readjust my thinking *and* my feelings:

1. **Develop a mature view of suffering.**

   Because I live in a fallen world, I am quickly influenced by the world's view of the relationship between suffering and joy. We're told that they are polar opposites, but the truth is, there can be joy in suffering. When we meet God in the dark places and He gets us through, we can feel the joy of His presence. We can also feel joy when we realize that we are progressing spiritually as we face our fears, even when doing so is hard. A mature woman realizes that suffering can't be avoided, and if we never encountered it, there would be a lot of life lessons missed.

2. **Grow in faith and trust.**

   Faith and trust are the antidotes to fear. I'm so glad that we can ask God to give us more faith when we feel we are lacking. When we stay close to the Lord and exercise the little faith we do have, He waters that seed of faith and makes it grow. When I focus on how God has been faithful to me in the past, I grow in trust.

   It's been helpful for me to keep a prayer journal so that I can go back and see the ways God has rescued me and given me what I have needed countless times. When I read the Bible, I get to know God better, which helps me see that He is worthy of my trust. I won't trust someone I don't know. If we want to grow in trust, we have to take the time to get to know God personally.

3. **Remember that I am never alone.**

   This comforts me most of all. Jesus has suffered more than I ever will, so He knows how I am feeling. The Bible promises that no matter what happens to me, God has made sure I can endure it (1 Corinthians 10:13). But He doesn't say I'll be able to handle anything in my own strength. I will have to cling to Him in order to receive the strength I need, just as a small branch clings to the main vine.

   What is it that you most fear? Can you write it here?

Then write a prayer asking for God's help. You might want to affirm your trust in God's goodness and His control over all things, and thank Him for His wise plan for your life.

Dear God,

My Resolution

In what specific way will I apply what I have learned in this lesson?

1. When my fears are getting the better of me, I will make a Trust List. This is a list of ways in which I know I can trust God. It can contain words describing His character, or descriptions of times when He has proven to be faithful in the midst of my struggles. I'll reread this list (or make a new one) whenever I need a reminder.

2. I'll memorize one of the verses from this week's lesson. This will allow the Holy Spirit to bring it to my mind when I most need it.

3. I'll experience the shelter and safety of God's presence by spending some time this week at adoration.

My resolution:

Catechism Clip

CCC 227 [The implications of Faith in One God:] It means trusting God in every circumstance, even in adversity. A prayer of St. Teresa of Jesus wonderfully expresses this trust:

> Let nothing trouble you / Let nothing frighten you
> Everything passes / God never changes
> Patience / Obtains all
> Whoever has God / Wants for nothing
> God alone is enough.

Lesson 3

UNSHACKLED ~ EXPERIENCING REAL TRANSFORMATION

Introduction

"I can't kick that habit. It's just too ingrained in me."
"Worrying is in my nature. It's how I process things."
"I know I drink more than I should, but I need it to take the edge off."
"I can't help the way I fly off the handle."
"I can never lose weight."
"I can't change. This is how God made me."

It probably wouldn't take us very long to make a list of things we'd like to change about ourselves. I sure would love to break free of my fear of failure and the fact that my default coping mechanism is perfectionism and performance. That would be so fantastic. The weight of the world just might lift off my shoulders. But when I'm asked if I believe it's possible for these changes to occur, I can quickly feel discouraged. I hear other people's success stories, but all too often I doubt that this level of radical transformation could happen to me.

Can you relate? Perhaps you've prayed for God to help you, but you're still stuck in the same rut. Has it caused you to wonder if God cares? Do your spirits lift at the thought that God's unconditional love means you're OK just as you are, but then deflate at the thought of never being free from the habits that keep you in bondage?

While it's true that God loves us unconditionally, He loves us too much to leave us as we are. He knows that the sins that disfigure us are keeping us from the abundant life He created us for. And He knows that Christians walking around looking no different than people who don't have Christ in their lives is not the way it's supposed to be. We are promised in 2 Corinthians 5:17, "If anyone is in Christ he is a new creation. The old is gone, the new has come." A *new creation* is a picture of freedom—a beautiful butterfly that has emerged from a cocoon after metamorphosis.

When we feel stuck, we are forgetting the secret of the Christian life: **The same power that conquered the grave lives in you!** This means that there is *always* hope for change.

In 1 Corinthians 3:16, Saint Paul asks, "Do you not know that you are the temple of God, and that the Spirit of God dwells in you?"

Then in Romans 8:11, Saint Paul writes about the difference the indwelling Holy Spirit makes: "If the Spirit of the one who raised Jesus from the dead dwells in you, the one who raised Christ from the dead will give life to your mortal bodies also, through his Spirit that dwells in you."

This means that the Holy Spirit *in you* wants to bring new life to places you have long felt were dead. He wants to radically change you from the inside out. And He's got the power to do it. This week we're going to look at four steps that'll help us to move toward becoming the women we long to be.

Day One
ADMIT THAT THERE'S A PROBLEM

Step 1 is admitting that the area where you want to change is actually a problem. It's not a "thorn in the flesh" that you're expected to live with forever, and it's not a quirky part of your personality. This is something that God wants you to be free of.

1. List an area of your life where you would like to see transformation. Is this something friends and family believe you have a problem with? Is it impacting your relationships with others? Do you try to hide this problem from people? Can you go without engaging in this behavior for a week? Do you arrange parts of your life (your schedule, your spending) around it? Answering these questions can give an indication of how strong a hold the problem has on you. Be honest with yourself; you're the only one reading this.

2. A. What does Romans 6:14 tell us about the power of sin?

    B. According to this passage, if we're no longer under the law, what are we under?

When the Bible says that we are "not under law but under grace," it's referring to our position as daughters of God—as Christians. This position is described in the footnotes of the Ignatius Catholic Study Bible as follows:

> *under grace:* The new position of the believer, who can master the urges of sin with the assistance of God. This inward strength to suppress our fallen inclinations was a grace not yet available to Israel living under the yoke of the Law.

Because we are under grace, we can master the urge to sin. We can be changed. The law had the power to point out the way people were to live, but it totally lacked the power to help people to actually obey. Everything radically changed when Jesus was raised from the dead, breaking the chains of death.

We talk a lot about what the cross accomplished. Jesus' sacrifice allowed us to be totally forgiven; He paid the price for our sin in full. But the Resurrection—that's where our freedom was really won. That's when Jesus broke through all the things that keep us dead, bound, and defeated. He was victorious over it all—He *was* and *is* stronger than it all—and He wants us to walk in the freedom He won for us.

3. What has set us free from the law of sin and death? See Romans 8:2.

The "law of the Spirit" is the power of grace at work in our lives.

God knows we feel a continual pull toward sin—it's the pull to take the easy way out, to value the wrong things, to make the selfish choice. Knowing that's the human condition, He steps in and pours divine love into our hearts so we can resist temptation. He places His very own Spirit, the Holy Spirit, into our hearts so that we have power within to slay the dragons that seek to keep us in bondage.

Quiet your heart and enjoy His presence. . . . You'll find grace and mercy—not condemnation.

I believe it's easier to face our problems—to call them what they really are: sins, addictions, idols—when we believe that freedom from them is possible. So lean in close and listen: God does not want you to stay in this place. He is just waiting to help you experience freedom and victory. But it has to start with you. It has to begin with you acknowledging that your behavior is hurting you—and probably people close to you. It has to begin with you admitting that this ingrained habit isn't something that you can control in your own strength. You are at a crossroads. You can choose to face the need to change or you can ignore it. But hasn't it been heavy to carry this load? Aren't you tired of the price you pay? God wants to lift this burden from you. He lovingly waits to be invited into the struggle.

Write a prayer to the Lord in the space provided, telling Him that you want to be free. Name the problem and ask Him for His help. Trust that as you spill out your struggle in His presence, He is whispering over you, "I love you. I love you. I love you."

Day Two
ASK FOR GOD'S HELP

Really coming to terms with our need to change—naming a problem that requires a solution—is the first step toward freedom. The next is to invite God into the process. As good as this sounds in theory, it isn't our typical response. Most of us begin to address a problem by getting to work and searching for solutions. This is trying to change in our own strength, and all too often, we'll fail to see real transformation. We are promised in Mark 10:27 that "with man, this is impossible—but not with God; all things are possible with God." We aren't promised that all things are possible in *our own* strength. In fact, in John 15:5, we are told, "apart from [God] we can do nothing."

There's a big difference between saying we're going to pray about something and then actually doing it. Hopefully the verses we study today will motivate us to live out Colossians 1:29: "To this end I labor, struggling with all *his* energy, which so powerfully works in me" (emphasis added).

Unshackled ~ Experiencing Real Transformation | 3

Read 2 Corinthians 10:3–5.

1. This passage talks about a battle. As we battle toward freedom from sin, God gives us weapons to help us fight. How are they described in 2 Corinthians 10:3–4?

2. The weapons of our battle are capable of destroying three specific things mentioned in this passage. What are they?

3. In the original Greek, the word *fortress* describes the place a person goes to seek shelter (a safe place) or to escape reality. When we think of battling to break free of habits and sins that have a grip on us, it's helpful to consider them fortresses that need to be destroyed. Why do we continue to do these things that we know ultimately harm us and those we love? Sometimes we're trying to escape reality. Sometimes we fool ourselves into thinking that these behaviors or coping mechanisms are helping us to be more in control of things. Whatever our reason, the very thing we think will bring us greater control ends up having control over us. On our own, we can't get out from under them. But with the weapons God gives us, freedom can be won.

   Do you recognize this pattern in your own life? As you identify the area where you desire to change—to experience freedom—has it been a place where you have gone to escape? Or has it been something that has caused you to feel more in control?

4. The weapons of our battle also equip us to destroy "arguments and every pretension raising itself against the knowledge of God." This is referring to the

outward reasoning and inward pride that convince us that we don't need God—that we can solve our problems on our own. This isn't just a battle "out there" in our messed-up world. This is a problem that goes on within us. Do you recognize this tendency in yourself? Have you experienced this pull toward self-sufficiency?

Quiet your heart and enjoy His presence. . . . You need Him; an earnest desire to change is not all it takes.

We have got to get rid of the illusion that we have it within us to break down the fortresses that keep us from freedom. We have got to let go of our pride that says it's all up to us. When we're talking about deep-seated issues, long-held patterns of behavior, and addictions, we have got to have weapons that are powerful enough for the battle. The weapons God gives us allow us to fight in the spiritual dimension. It adds supernatural power to our resolve, self-discipline, and determination.

Spend some time talking to God about your need for His help. Invite Him into the struggle. Ask His forgiveness for running to fortresses instead of running to Him. Ask Him to forgive you for any pride that has caused you to rely on yourself instead of Him. Ask Him to break through any barriers that are keeping you away from a life of freedom.

Note: In no way am I suggesting that professional help is unnecessary as we battle addiction. I am making the point that pursuing freedom apart from God means that we miss out on supernatural power that can make all the difference in the world. Going to God first does not mean that we don't also take advantage of other resources available.

Day Three
PUT ON YOUR ARMOR AND PICK UP YOUR WEAPONS

What provisions does God give us for the spiritual battle? In Ephesians 6, we read about both the defensive armor and the offensive weapons at our disposal. As we engage in the battle to experience true freedom, we're to draw our "strength from the Lord and from his mighty power" (Ephesians 6:10). We do this by putting on the armor of God, picking up our weapons, and using them.

1. A. Describe the armor of God from Ephesians 6:13–17.

   The Belt of Truth: When God's truth surrounds us, we are protected from lies that keep us from living as beloved daughters of God. The lies say, "I can't. I'll never change." The Truth says, "With God, all things are possible" (Mark 10:27).

   The Breastplate of Righteousness: Greek historian Polybius described the breastplate that covered the soldier from the neck to the thigh as "the heart protector." A holy life protects the most vital part of us: the soul. Self-discipline is like a muscle—the more it gets exercised, the stronger it becomes. There is protection in obedience.

   Feet Fitted with the Gospel: A soldier's shoes had nails or spikes in the sole to help him stand firmly and keep his balance. In that same way, the gospel gives us something solid to stand on. We don't stand on the foundation of our own perfection. We stand on the truth of Christ's perfect sacrifice having paid the price for our sins. He makes up for where we are lacking.

   The Shield of Faith: We put up the shield of faith to protect ourselves from the fiery darts of doubt, fear, discouragement, and condemnation. Our prayer becomes, "I believe; help my disbelief!" (Mark 9:24). God faithfully strengthens our faith when we ask Him to.

   The Helmet of Salvation: The helmet protects the brain. When we focus on the gift of salvation, our minds are protected from thoughts of worthlessness and hopelessness. We remember that we are worth *everything* to Jesus.

   The Sword of the Spirit: The sword of the Spirit is an offensive weapon. This is Scripture, and the more we know it, the more we can use it to gain ground spiritually instead of just treading water and staying in the same place. When we memorize Scripture, the Holy Spirit can bring God's truth to our minds just when we need to fight temptation or negative thoughts.

   B. Do you wear this armor? Are there some pieces that you forget to put on each day?

2. The sword of the Spirit (Scripture) is the first offensive weapon mentioned in this passage. What is the second offensive weapon? See Ephesians 6:18.

Prayer ensures that we have a constant supply of the grace and help we need to resist temptation. It calls down the help of heaven and makes all the difference in the world. Prayer should never be our last resort, because battles are won when we fight on our knees.

3. The sacraments are essential weapons that allow us to battle the constant pull toward mediocrity and compromise. Read each of the following quotes or passages, and record your thoughts regarding how God uses the sacraments to help you change and live as "a new creation" (2 Corinthians 5:17) in Christ. Do you take advantage of all that the sacraments offer you?

   A. **CCC 1266** The Most Holy Trinity gives the baptized sanctifying grace, the grace of justification:

   -enabling them to believe in God, to hope in him, and to love him through the theological virtues;
   -giving them the power to live and act under the prompting of the Holy Spirit through the gifts of the Holy Spirit;
   -allowing them to grow in goodness through the moral virtues.

   Thus the whole organism of the Christian's supernatural life has its roots in **Baptism**.

   B. **CCC 1394** As bodily nourishment restores lost strength, so **the Eucharist** strengthens our charity, which tends to be weakened in daily life; and this living charity wipes away venial sins. By giving himself to us Christ revives our love and enables us to break our disordered attachments to creatures and root ourselves in him.

C. "Satan tempts us to deny responsibility for our sins. Our only defense is to take responsibility for them. The only weapon that can defeat the Prince of Darkness is light. That is the purpose of the **Sacrament of Penance**. The priest in the confessional is a more formidable foe to the devil than an exorcist."[18] —Peter Kreeft

Quiet your heart and enjoy His presence. . . . He is waiting to outfit you for battle.

Dear Lord,

Please cover me with the armor of God.

*Buckle the **belt of truth** around my waist. You are truth, so wrap yourself around me and help me to dwell on what is true.*

*I take the **breastplate of righteousness** from your hand and thank you for giving me your righteousness. Help me to stay protected by your grace by making the right choices today.*

*Place the **helmet of salvation** on my head and protect my mind.*

*May my **feet be shod by the gospel**. Everywhere I go today, may I spread that message.*

*Oil my **shield of faith** with the Holy Spirit so that all the fiery darts flung at me will be extinguished.*

*I take up the **sword of the Spirit**. Let me be ready to fight back any lies with the truth found in Scripture.*

Amen.

---

[18] Peter Kreeft, *Catholic Christianity: A Complete Catechism of Catholic Beliefs Based on the Catechism of the Catholic Church* (San Francisco: Ignatius Press, 2001).

Day Four
WALK AWAY FROM THE QUICKSAND

There's no question that God gives us everything we need to resist temptation. While He certainly equips us for battle, there are some battles He wants us to just walk away from. These are the battles on top of quicksand, and the only way to win is to avoid the area completely. This is essentially the message of Romans 6: You are free from the grip of sin, *so walk away from it*.

1. Read 1 Corinthians 15:33 and reflect on your choice of friends. Do some of your friends encourage you to live the way God wants you to? Do others consistently draw you into behavior that you later regret? Is God asking you to change where you are spending your time?

We are wise to be discerning in choosing our friends, because as it says in Proverbs 13:20, "He who walks with the wise grows wise, but a companion of fools suffers harm." No matter how strong our personality or how well we know ourselves, we are always influenced by our friends. Even Jesus gave careful thought to choosing His friends. He spent all night in prayer before selecting His twelve disciples, asking God to help Him discern whom He should surround Himself with.

2. According to Colossians 3:1–10, what are we to be seeking and setting our mind on? What should we be "putting to death" within us? Which of these behaviors is like quicksand for you? What do you need to walk away from?

3. How is "the way of perfection" described in CCC 2015?

Quiet your heart and enjoy His presence. . . . Walk away from the quicksand and run toward the One who gives you life.

There's no growth in holiness without battling temptation and walking away from situations that are sure to take us down. It involves a thousand little deaths. It's hard, and requires grit and sacrifice. Through it all, we're called to persevere. As Saint Gregory of Nyssa said, "He who climbs never stops going." The journey isn't easy, but the destination makes it all worth it.

Dear Lord,

This is where the rubber meets the road. As long as I don't feel equipped to change, I feel like I don't have to. I have an excuse. In John 5:6, you asked the man lying by the pool in Bethesda, "Do you want to be well?" The man replied with an excuse. He was so used to being crippled that all he could think of were the reasons he'd never get better. And there you stood, with all the power imaginable at your disposal, ready to help. You looked at the man and said, "Rise, take up your mat, and walk."

I know that you ask me the same question. "Do you really want to be well?" It's time for me to stop making excuses and to grasp hold of your promise from Philippians 4:13: "I can do all things through Christ who strengthens me." It's time for me to pick up my mat and walk—to walk toward freedom. No more excuses. I want to be well.

Day Five
SAINT'S STORY

Saint Monica Outlasts the Devil

Two of the most difficult Christian virtues are patience and perseverance. Having patience means elegantly putting up with persistent difficulties—especially one's own personality flaws and selfish tendencies. Having perseverance means maintaining the struggle to overcome obstacles (especially those same flaws and tendencies) no matter how long it takes or how hard it gets. At times we are tempted to get discouraged because we don't see results right away. But discouragement never comes from God. What seems a long time to us is only a heartbeat to Him, and what seems like slow or no progress to us may be yielding abundant fruit in ways we cannot see. "But do not ignore this one fact, beloved, that with the Lord one day is like a thousand years and a thousand years like one day. The Lord does not delay his promise, as some regard 'delay,' but he is patient with you, not wishing that any should perish but that all should come to repentance" (2 Peter 3:8–9). God hears every prayer and values every effort, as Saint Monica can attest. She is a model of Christ's own love coursing through our hearts—the reason why true Christians can find the strength to be heroically patient and persevere amazingly. And Christ's love never, ever gives up. It dies on the cross instead, and then rises again.

Monica spent almost twenty years pleading with God through tears and entreaties to bring her wayward son into the Christian fold. At times she spent entire nights in prayer. More often than not, when she allowed herself a few hours of rest, she cried herself to sleep. She had grown up a Christian in northern Africa in the 400s, but had married a pagan. Her husband tolerated her faith, although his temper and dissolute living (as well as his mother, who was a most disagreeable person and resided with them) caused her constant grief and difficulty. Eventually, however, her prayers and Christian example won both her husband and her mother-in-law over to the faith a year before her husband's death. At about that time, their eldest son was finishing his elite education and notified his mother that he had embraced Manichaeism (a heresy). Nothing could have pained her more. She spared no effort to save him, arranging meetings for him with eminent churchmen, arguing with him herself, disciplining him by taking away family privileges, and always, day after day, year after year, praying for him. Only after she had pursued him to Rome and Milan, where the rebellious Augustine (who had meanwhile taken up residence with a mistress and fathered an illegitimate child) finally met his match in Saint Ambrose, was her prayer answered. Augustine, the future Bishop of Hippo, saint, and Doctor of the Church, was baptized while she looked on, her eyes overflowing with tears and her heart overflowing with gratitude.

She stuck it out. Why? Because she loved. Love simply can't give up. When we truly love Christ, we keep going, knowing that since He truly loves us, all our efforts will eventually bear wonderful fruit for us and for those around us. One of the many lessons that Saint Monica taught her son was precisely that: unlimited confidence in the transforming power of God's love. When Augustine left North Africa (after abandoning his Christian faith), he did so in secret so that his mother wouldn't go with him (she actually wanted him to stay because she feared he would drift further away from the truth if he traveled to Italy).

Here is Saint Augustine's later reflection on that incident:

> Why I left the one country and went to the other, you knew, O God, but you did not tell either me or my mother. She indeed was in dreadful grief at my going and followed me right to the seacoast.... That night I stole away without her; she remained praying and weeping. And what was she praying for, O my God, with all those tears but that you should not allow me to sail! But you saw deeper and granted the essential part of her prayer: you did not do

what she was at that moment asking, that you might do the thing she was always asking.

As you read Saint Monica's story, consider how she embodied the virtues of patience and perseverance as she prayed for her son to experience spiritual transformation. What lessons have you learned this week to help you persevere in your journey toward holiness?

Conclusion

"When Christians stop being different from the world and instead fall back into their old habits, it is as tragic as finding a royal prince sleeping out on the streets in a gutter, having forgotten he belongs in the palace."[19] —Adrian Warnock

You are God's beloved daughter, a child of the King of kings. He doesn't want you lying on a mat, crippled by sin. He offers you His hand, invites you to get up and walk with Him toward the freedom of holiness.

Holiness is within reach. It isn't beyond you. This isn't a call to live in a constant state of fear, afraid of disappointing God or making Him angry. It's an invitation from your heavenly Father, who is *good*, who is *for you*, and who gives you the power of the Holy Spirit. This power breaks the chains of addiction, destructive habits, and behaviors that hurt us.

It's counterintuitive, but we are actually blessed when we come to the end of our resources— when our self-reliance proves to be insufficient. This brings us to a place where we are far more likely to ask God for help. You can't change in your own power. If you feel overwhelmed at the thought of breaking free of sins that have long held you in their grasp, then turn to the One who is bigger than all things. He will be strong in your weakness.

God has given you everything you need in order to live your life the way He desires. He's given you His very presence in your soul. The Holy Spirit fills you with love, joy, peace, patience, kindness, goodness, faithfulness, gentleness, and self-control. If those are the things you need, you can't say you don't have them. It's just that we often don't tap into the power that is within us. God has given us the sacraments to fill us with His grace, which is exactly what we need for whatever we face.

---

[19] Adrian Warnock, *Raised with Christ: How the Resurrection Changes Everything* (Wheaton, IL: Crossway Books, 2010), 143.

"Do not be afraid to be holy! Have the courage and humility to present yourselves to the world determined to be holy, since full, true freedom is born from holiness." — Saint John Paul II

My Resolution

In what specific way will I apply what I have learned in this lesson?

Examples:

1. If I need professional help with an addiction, I will make an appointment to talk with someone this week.

2. I will receive the sacrament of penance this week, recognizing that when I do this, God deals a blow to the sin that has been gripping me. I'm not only forgiven; I receive power to resist temptation in the future.

3. I've recognized that some of my friendships are not leading me in the right direction. I'll make a concerted effort to build a relationship with a woman whose character is the type I would like to reflect.

My resolution:

Catechism Clips

CCC 1394 As bodily nourishment restores lost strength, so the Eucharist strengthens our charity, which tends to be weakened in daily life; and this living charity wipes away venial sins. By giving himself to us Christ revives our love and enables us to break our disordered attachments to creatures and root ourselves in him.

> Since Christ died for us out of love, when we celebrate the memorial of his death at the moment of sacrifice we ask that love may be granted to us by the

coming of the Holy Spirit. We humbly pray that in the strength of this love by which Christ willed to die for us, we by receiving the gift of the Holy Spirit, may be able to consider the world as crucified for us, and to be ourselves as crucified to the world. . . . Having received the gift of love, let us die to sin and live for God.

CCC 1266 The Most Holy Trinity gives the baptized sanctifying grace, the grace of justification:

-enabling them to believe in God, to hope in him, and to love him through the theological virtues;

-giving them the power to live and act under the prompting of the Holy Spirit through the gifts of the Holy Spirit;

-allowing them to grow in goodness through the moral virtues.

Thus the whole organism of the Christian's supernatural life has its roots in Baptism.

CCC 2015 The way of perfection passes by way of the Cross. There is no holiness without renunciation and spiritual battle. Spiritual progress entails the ascesis and mortification that gradually leads to living in the peace and joy of the Beatitudes: "He who climbs never stops going from beginning to beginning, through beginnings that have no end. He never stops desiring what he already knows." (Saint Gregory of Nyssa)

NOTES

No program near you? No problem...it's easy to start your own group in your parish or at home and we will walk with you every step of the way. Find out more:

www.walkingwithpurpose.com/leadership

Lesson 4

VALIANT ~ SUFFERING WITH PURPOSE

Introduction

I have stood beside a beloved friend when she was in the midst of unthinkable suffering, and I don't know when I have ever felt more helpless. My words couldn't bring healing. I could hold her but I couldn't prevent her from falling into despair. I felt the howl of her soul but could do nothing to lessen the pain.

I've felt the weight of suffering myself, and have wondered if I would come out the other side whole, or if I would be crushed underneath it all.

Saint Teresa of Ávila's words, "Dear Lord, if this is how you treat your friends, it is no wonder you have so few," have resonated with me.

As we step into this lesson on suffering, I must acknowledge that I don't know your story. I don't know the pain you've endured in the past, or the suffering you might be experiencing in this very moment. And I recognize that when we come to this subject, we are treading on sacred ground. This is the place where people quoting Bible verses often inflict pain more than they bring comfort. I don't know about you, but when I am in the vise grip of suffering, I don't really want to hear someone whose life looks a heck of a lot easier than mine quoting Romans 8:28: "We know that all things work for good for those who love God, who are called according to his purpose."

But I don't want to drown in my pain, either. And if there is comfort and hope to be had in the midst of it all, I want it. Oh, how I long for that.

The Lord draws near to us in our pain, and whispers in our ears, "I am close to the brokenhearted and save those who are crushed in spirit" (Psalm 34:19, NAB).

He is true to His word. He never fails to keep His promises. But notice what He *doesn't* promise. Nowhere in Scripture does He promise to be our genie or errand boy. He isn't our servant.

When we encounter suffering, nothing robs us of peace like expectations. During this lesson, we're going to focus on four of those expectations and see if we can come to a deeper understanding of the role of suffering in our lives.

Day One
EXPECTATION 1: WE EXPECT TO UNDERSTAND GOD

We have questions. Suffering intersects our lives and our hearts cry out to know *why*. Some of us are angry, and we want God to give an explanation of what He has allowed or even caused. Some of us aren't angry, but we are deeply disillusioned. We just can't bear the senselessness of it all. The unanswered questions feel intolerable. Life around us feels chaotic sometimes, and we silently question, "How can a loving God be *in charge* if this is what it all feels like?"

1. What insight do the following verses shed on our expectation that we will understand God and His plans?

    Isaiah 55:8–9

    Proverbs 3:5

2. When will we fully understand "the ways of God's providence"? See CCC 314.

3. In his work as a licensed psychologist and a marriage, family, and child counselor, Dr. James Dobson has witnessed the impact of suffering on people's faith. He has this to say about what causes the most difficulty during crushing circumstances:

It is an incorrect view of Scripture to say that we will always comprehend what God is doing and how our suffering and disappointment fit into His plan. Sooner or later, most of us will come to a point where it appears that God has lost control—or interest—in the affairs of people. It is only an illusion, but one with dangerous implications for spiritual and mental health. **Interestingly enough, pain and suffering do not cause the greatest damage. Confusion is the factor that shreds one's faith . . .** The human spirit is capable of withstanding enormous discomfort, including the prospect of death, *if the circumstances make sense.*[20]

Do you agree or disagree with Dr. Dobson's observation? Have you experienced this in your own life?

4. According to Psalm 9:11, NAB, how are the people who trust in God described?

"Knowing God's name" signifies knowing something about who God is. A name has great significance in the Bible; it goes beyond being something that sounds nice or has some sentimental value. In the Bible, a name represents the worth, character, and authority of a person. When someone knows God's name, it means that he or she has taken the time to know Him intimately. When we *know* Him, we can base our trust on His character, instead of on our ability to understand our suffering.

Quiet your heart and enjoy His presence. . . . He is so great that it's impossible for us to wrap our minds around Him, yet He stoops low and draws near.

---

[20] Dr. James Dobson, *When God Doesn't Make Sense* (Wheaton, IL: Tyndale House, 1993), 13.

The essence of who God is can be grasped in a small yet faith-building way by studying the names of God. As you read these Hebrew names, focus on God's character and ask the Lord to help your trust in Him grow.

El Shaddai (Lord God Almighty)
El Elyon (The Most High God)
Jehovah-Raah (The Lord My Shepherd)
Jehovah-Rapha (The Lord That Heals)
Jehovah Shammah (The Lord Is There)
Jehovah Mekoddishkem (The Lord Who Makes You Holy)
Jehovah Jireh (The Lord Will Provide)
Jehovah Shalom (The Lord Is Peace)

God doesn't promise us an answer to our whys, but He promises something better: His presence.

"He will stand and shepherd his flock
in the strength of the lord,
in the majesty of the name of the lord his God.
And they will live securely, for then his greatness
will reach to the ends of the earth.
And he will be our peace." (Micah 5:3–4, NAB)

Day Two
EXPECTATION 2: WE EXPECT GOD'S DEFINITION OF HAPPINESS TO BE THE SAME AS OURS

It seems so straightforward to us. We know that good relationships, health, financial security, and blessings on our loved ones will make us happy. We read over that list and assume that since none of those things are bad, they must be the very things that God considers good sources of happiness. And when things go wrong, we feel perplexed. We wonder if God cares if we are happy or not. We start to question His goodness and whether or not He truly wants what is best for us. As a result, our trust in God starts to take a beating, and our hearts grow cold and disillusioned. We blame God, because if He's all-powerful, then He is able to give us any and all of these things. Yet He holds back just what we are certain would make things all right again.

We become convinced that the problem lies in having something we don't want or wanting something we don't have. But open your mind to another possibility—could it be that the real problem lies in our understanding of what true happiness is?

1. *The Merriam-Webster Dictionary* defines happiness as "a state of well-being and contentment: joy." Read the following verses and record what Scripture says will bring us joy.

   Psalm 16:11

   James 1:2

   1 Peter 1:8–9

2. It has been said that joy comes from obedience. When we understand how God wants us to live and then we obey Him no matter the cost, we experience the joy of pleasing Him. God knows what will bring us to "a state of well-being and contentment." As hard as it is to accept, He knows better than we do. What we think will bring us happiness today might be the very thing that will keep us from experiencing happiness in eternity. Because of this, we are called to obey even when we don't understand why. Is there an area of your life where God has asked you to obey Him and you're finding it hard to do? Share the struggle here. Then read Hebrews 12:2. What helped Jesus to obediently go to the cross even though it meant abject suffering?

The world says happiness is found through pleasure. God says happiness is found through obedience.

3. If we make the source of our happiness the temporal things of this world, at any given point we can be made unhappy, because those things can be taken away from us. God wants us to experience a deeper kind of happiness, a joy that can't be taken away. What did Jesus promise about joy in John 16:22?

The promise Jesus made to His disciples in John 16:22 is also true for us today. He rose from the dead, and because of this, we are assured of His presence here on earth.

He will never leave us. We're also promised joy in heaven—eternal joy—where Jesus "will wipe every tear from [our] eyes, and there shall be no more death or mourning, wailing or pain" (Revelation 21:4).

Quiet your heart and enjoy His presence. . . . "Many say, 'May we see better times! LORD, show us the light of your face!' But you have given my heart more joy than they have when grain and wine abound. In peace I will lie down and fall asleep, for you alone, LORD, make me secure" (Psalm 4:7–9, NAB).

True happiness comes from more than "grain and wine abounding." It's found in God's presence. Our security and joy lie in Him, not in our circumstances. Whether our relationships are peaceful or full of conflict, whether our finances are in great shape or not, whether our loved ones are suffering or experiencing smooth sailing, we are safe and secure in Christ.

"What has happened to all your joy?" (Galatians 4:15)

Could it be that you've been looking for it in the wrong place?

Day Three
EXPECTATION 3: WE EXPECT GOD'S LOVE TO ALWAYS FEEL GOOD

Nothing feels better than a police officer giving me grace when I deserve a speeding ticket. My family thinks I have perfected the art of crying under duress. I just think the police officer is caught off guard when I say, "You were so right to pull me over. I totally deserve a ticket." You are free to borrow this technique in your own hour of need.

Each and every time I've been pulled over, the officer has checked my record, seen a clean slate, and let me go with a warning. He of course has no idea how many warnings I've received. Bless. *And I am grateful.* That being said, do you know what I probably *need*? I probably need a whopping ticket to teach me that there is no reason to speed and that we have speed limits for our protection. Getting away with speeding feels good in the moment, but it doesn't really help me to slow down.

(And I hope that there aren't any police officers living near me reading this. Because even when I know what is best for me, I don't really want it if it doesn't feel good. So just in case you thought I was writing about these things from a high and lofty place of holiness, be assured, I'm right smack in the middle of the mess with you.)

What happens when we expect God's love to always feel good? Suffering, which is meant to help us and teach us something, ends up making us bitter. That root of bitterness goes down deep into our hearts, and we start to question God's character. That's not all. We get stuck there. Instead of growing up in our faith, we become perpetual adolescents. Let's take a look at what God's love feels like when He is in the process of making His beloved daughters more closely resemble His Son.

1. Read Hebrews 12:5–11 and answer the following questions.

   A. Whom does the Lord discipline? (see verse 6)

   B. Why does the Lord discipline us? (see verse 10)

   C. Discipline will bring "the peaceful fruit of righteousness" to whom? (see verse 11)

We don't all experience "the peaceful fruit of righteousness"; it doesn't automatically accompany discipline and suffering. Some people who've been through a lot wear their suffering as a badge. We notice it, and there is always a certain amount of respect we give to someone who has endured something terribly difficult. But the holiness we're after isn't the same thing as wearing a badge of suffering. We need to be refined by what we experience. It's not *that* you've suffered; it's *how* you've suffered that really matters.

2. Left to our own devices, all too often we will choose temporary comfort over what will ultimately benefit us most. C. S. Lewis points this out in the following excerpt from his book *The Problem of Pain*:

   > Everyone has noticed how hard it is to turn our thoughts to God when everything is going well with us. "We have all we want" is a terrible saying when "all" does not include God. We find God an interruption. As St. Augustine says somewhere, "God wants to give us something, but cannot,

because our hands are full—there's nowhere for Him to put it." Or as a friend of mine said, "We regard God as an airman regards his parachute; it's there for emergencies but he hopes he'll never have to use it." Now God, who has made us, knows what we are and that our happiness lies in Him. Yet we will not seek it in Him as long as He leaves us any other resort where it can even plausibly be looked for. While what we call "our own life" remains agreeable we will not surrender it to Him. What then can God do in our interests but make our own life less agreeable to us, and take away the plausible source of false happiness? It is just here, where God's providence seems at first to be most cruel, that the Divine humility, the stepping down of the Highest, most deserves praise.[21]

Underline any phrases from the excerpt that resonate with you. Do C. S. Lewis' words give you any insight into why your loving God has allowed suffering in your life?

3. Even though I know that a speeding ticket would help me to slow down, I don't want the correction. This is a common human tendency that it seems I share with C. S. Lewis (and unfortunately that's about where our similarities end). In *The Problem of Pain*, he writes of the way in which suffering has grabbed his attention. Suffering causes him to realize that his greatest treasure is Christ and that there is nothing more important than being utterly dependent on Him. But as soon as his suffering lifts, Lewis observes that he goes right back to trying to fill himself up with life's little pleasures. He continues with the following words:

> Thus the terrible necessity of tribulation is only too clear. God has had me for but forty-eight hours and then only by dint of taking everything else away from me. Let Him but sheathe that sword for a moment and I behave like a puppy when the hated bath is over—I shake myself as dry as I can and race off to reacquire my comfortable dirtiness, if not in the nearest manure heap, at least in the nearest flower bed. And that is why tribulations cannot cease until God either sees us remade or sees that our remaking is now hopeless.[22]

---

[21] C. S. Lewis, *The Problem of Pain* (New York: HarperCollins, 2001), 94.
[22] Ibid.

Do you relate to this? Can you see this tendency in yourself to return to the "comfortable dirtiness" of old habits?

Quiet your heart and enjoy His presence. . . . His discipline is proof not that you are bad, but that you are beloved.

"My [daughter], do not despise the LORD's discipline or be weary of his reproof, for the LORD reproves [her] whom he loves, as a father the [daughter] in whom he delights." (Proverbs 3:11–12)

God loves you so very, very much. You are His beloved daughter, and He wants you to resemble your brother Jesus. He knows that the more you are like Jesus, not just in outward actions but deep in your heart, the more happy and fulfilled you will be. He knows that this refining process is absolutely essential if you are going to walk in the freedom you were created for. Have you resisted the discipline of your heavenly Father? Let today be the start of a new attitude toward the difficulties He allows to come your way. Instead of responding to them with the words, "Why me, Lord?" change the response to, "Father, what are you trying to teach me?"

Day Four
EXPECTATION 4: WE EXPECT TO SEE CLEAR EVIDENCE OF GOD WHEN WE NEED HIM

The rug is pulled out from under us and we need God like never before. We want to *see* Him. Yet He remains invisible, and we start to wonder, all this time that we've been loving, worshipping, and serving Him, is our God actually distant, uncaring, and silent? Doubts seep in like smoke, clouding our vision and causing us to wonder if we have any faith at all.

What do we do with these doubts? Are they signs that we don't have any faith? What do we do when we desperately want evidence that God is real, that God is there? Are we alone in this struggle?

1. Read Job 23:2–9 and underline every phrase that expresses Job's frustration over the hiddenness of God.

> Today especially my complaint is bitter, his hand is heavy upon me in my groanings. Would that I knew how to find him, that I might come to his dwelling! I would set out my case before him, fill my mouth with arguments; I would learn the words he would answer me, understand what he would say to me. Would he contend against me with his great power? No, he himself would heed me! There an upright man might argue with him, and I would once and for all be delivered from my judge. But if I go east, he is not there; or west, I cannot perceive him; the north enfolds him, and I cannot catch sight of him; the south hides him, and I cannot see him.

2. Read Psalm 13:2 and write it below. Have you ever felt like this? Record the experience here.

You are not alone in your struggle to see evidence of God in the midst of your suffering. You are not the only one who doubts. Struggling with doubt doesn't mean that you don't have faith. It can simply mean that you are in the midst of the process in which bit by bit you are learning to accept this:

God's greatness means that there will be times when you don't understand what He is doing, and you don't get to demand an explanation from Him. You are asked to trust, even when you can't see.

Are you wrestling with this? That's OK. It's totally different from giving up on God and closing off your heart to Him. Staying in the struggle is evidence of faith.

3. When we are having trouble seeing evidence of God in the midst of our suffering, we need to refocus on what we already know of Him. Record your thoughts on the following verses. Underline them in your Bible. Go back and reread these verses when doubts begin to creep into your heart.

Psalm 100:5

Valiant ~ Suffering with Purpose | 4

Romans 8:31–32

2 Peter 3:9

Quiet your heart and enjoy His presence. . . . He is real. He is here.

"Faith doesn't erase doubt, insecurity, or fear, it just overcomes them." —Jen Hatmaker

"In all these things, we conquer overwhelmingly through him who loved us. For I am convinced that neither death nor life, nor angels, nor principalities, nor present things, nor future things, nor powers, nor height, nor depth, nor any other creature will be able to separate us from the love of God in Christ Jesus our Lord." (Romans 8:37–39)

We can overcome doubt, insecurity, and fear. Inside each of us is God's very own Spirit. It's not a spirit of fear, but one of power and love (2 Timothy 1:7). The Spirit within us testifies that we are God's beloved daughters (Romans 8:16). Not only does the Lord go before and behind us, He is within us. God within us can do all things. Nothing is impossible. There is nothing He holds back from His daughters that is for their good.

God is for you. When all around you is shifting and misty and unclear, grab hold of that truth. When you're in the fire of suffering, shout into the flames that they are not going to overpower you, because God is in you and with you.

How do you arm wrestle? You grab hold of the other person's hand and you don't let go.

How do you wrestle with God? Grab hold of His hand. Don't let go. I promise you, He won't let go of you.

"For I am the LORD, your God, who grasp your right hand; It is I who say to you, Do not fear, I will help you." (Isaiah 41:13)

Day Five
SAINT'S STORY

Saint Rita of Cascia Fights the Good Fight

Following Christ is neither a hobby nor a game; it's an adventure. And every adventure worth the name is fraught with challenges, setbacks, threats, and enemies. This adventure is no exception. Christ needs us to grow in love so that His grace can take its full effect, both in our short life here on earth and in heaven for all eternity. But growth in love means perseverance through trials. Saint Paul assures us that God will never let us be tested beyond our strength: "You can trust that God will not let you be put to the test beyond your strength, but with any trial will also provide a way out by enabling you to put up with it" (1 Corinthians 10:13). But Saint Peter assures us that we will indeed be tested: "For a short time yet you must bear all sorts of trials" (1 Peter 1:6). And Saint James sums up the reason why: "My brothers, consider it a great joy when trials of many kinds come upon you, for you well know that the testing of your faith produces perseverance, and perseverance must complete its work so that you will become fully developed, complete, not deficient in any way" (James 1:2–4). Saint Rita had an especially grueling series of trials, which God used to turn her into a particularly remarkable and inspiring model of Christian womanhood.

Rita grew up in a little town in Central Italy during the early Renaissance. As all Italian towns were experiencing at the time, hers was torn by civil and political strife. Adverse conditions didn't impede the seed of faith from putting down deep roots in her soul, though, and early on she discovered her vocation to the religious life. Her parents, however, disagreed, and betrothed her to an abusive, violent, cantankerous man named Paolo, whom she married when she was twelve. For eighteen years she loved and served him faithfully, in spite of his infidelity and abuse. She bore him two sons, who spent their youth learning their father's ways.

These conditions tried her faith, and in the end strengthened it, as she saw that God had sent her this family so that she could pray and sacrifice for their salvation. Just before Paolo died (after being stabbed in an alley), he repented and begged his wife's forgiveness. And when the two sons vowed vengeance on their father's assassins, Rita prayed that they might die rather than commit murder. They fell ill (See how powerful prayer is?), and as their mother tended them, their hearts softened, and they, too, died in peace with God and man.

Because of the deaths of her husband and sons before she was even thirty-six years of age, Rita was able to pursue her heart's desire of dedicating her whole life to God. She applied various times for entrance into the local Augustinian convent. She was denied on multiple grounds (the order only admitted virgins; some members of the convent were relatives of the men who had killed Paolo), but she never gave up hope. In fact, she took action. She resolved the most salient family feuds in the town, achieving sufficient peace that it was considered safe to have her join the sisterhood, wherein she lived pursuing (and reaching) holiness for the next forty years.

Rita's love for Christ led her to a deep desire to share our Lord's suffering even more than she already had. He granted this desire in a rather unique way. One day in prayer, she was contemplating His Passion when she felt one of the thorns from His crown of thorns pierce her forehead. The wound turned out to be real. It bled and festered for the last sixteen years of her life, so much so that she had to live in seclusion in order to avoid revolting the other sisters. But during her final, bedridden years, the younger ones often stayed at her side to learn from her wisdom.

After her death, miracles abounded through her intercession, and to this day, she remains a patron saint for abuse victims, desperate causes, and difficult marriages. Her story reminds us that Christians, together with Christ, reach the joys of Easter Sunday only through the purifying struggles of Good Friday.

When you read Saint Rita's story, does a part of you feel mortified at the thought that this mother prayed that her sons would die rather than commit murder to avenge their father's death? Our response to Saint Rita's prayer reveals something about what we consider most important in life. We are tempted to live for the here and now instead of keeping our eyes fixed on heaven. The time we will spend on earth is such a tiny amount compared to eternity. We should live our lives in such a way that we can spend eternity with God. When we develop an eternal perspective, we take a different approach toward suffering. Even though the death of her sons would bring her suffering, Saint Rita trusted that God would bring a great good from that pain. Could it be that our struggle with the age-old question, "How can a good, loving God permit evil?" has a great deal to do with our lack of trust in God?

How does Saint Rita of Cascia's story add to your understanding of the suffering you have endured in your life?

Conclusion

No matter how faithfully we buckle our seat belts and lock our doors at night, we'll never be able to prevent suffering from intersecting our lives. How I wish I could promise you that if you love Jesus with all your heart, that heart will never break. But even the strongest faith and the presence of our Savior don't shield us from the effects of sin and evil in the world. Suffering comes into our lives, uninvited. So how will we be shaped by it? Will it form us into bitter, unforgiving, hardened women? Or will we be refined and come out the other side stronger, wiser, and more like Christ? The choice is ours. Even in the most horrific circumstances, the choice is still ours. No one says it better than WWII concentration camp survivor Viktor Frankl: "Everything can be taken from a man but one thing: the last of human freedoms—to choose one's attitude in any given set of circumstances, to choose one's own way."

No matter what you face, hold on to hope. Hold on to the promises of the God who loves you so much and will never let you go. Cling to these truths:

> God is **present** even when we feel that He isn't.
> God's timing is **perfect**.
> We are known and we are **precious** to Him.
> **Prayer** makes a difference.
> There is always a **purpose**.

That purpose is directly tied to God's greatest desire—to spend eternity with each person He lovingly created. Our life on earth is simply our journey toward that destination. And along the way, suffering is unquestionably one of the ways we are prepared to meet Him face-to-face. In the words of author Philip Yancey:

> The Bible consistently changes the questions we bring to the problem of pain. It rarely, or ambiguously, answers the backward-looking question "Why?" Instead, it raises the very different, forward-looking question, "To what end?" We are not put on earth merely to satisfy our desires,to pursue life, liberty, and happiness. We are here to be changed, to be made more like God in order to prepare us for a lifetime with Him. And that process may be served by the mysterious pattern of all creation: Pleasure sometimes emerges against a background of pain, evil may be transformed into good, and suffering may produce something of value.[23]

Let's live with our eyes fixed on eternity. Grasping hold of the moments of joy, let's see them as tastes of the utter fulfillment we'll experience in heaven. Let's check our expectations. Are we expecting life to be on earth what God promised us only in heaven?

---

[23] Philip Yancey, *Where Is God When It Hurts?* (Grand Rapids, MI: Zondervan, 1997), 88.

"Therefore, since we are surrounded by so great a cloud of witnesses, let us rid ourselves of every burden and sin that clings to us and persevere in running the race that lies before us... strengthen your dropping hands and your weak knees." (Hebrews 12:1, 12)

Run for that finish line with all you've got. And remember, it's not a sprint. It's a marathon. Stay steady and faithful, and press on through the pain. There is glory on the other side.

My Resolution

In what specific way will I apply what I have learned in this lesson?

1. I will think of one struggle in my life, and instead of asking God why, I will turn my question into a prayer: "God, how do you want me to respond when I struggle with this?" My prayer could sound something like this: "I am struggling in my relationship with _____. I want to ask you why I am going through this difficult time, but instead I'm asking you to show me how I should respond."

2. If I am struggling to believe that God is really *for me*, I will take time every morning to read Romans 8:31–32. I'll spend time really thinking about the significance of verse 32. How can I ever think that God is holding out on me when He didn't hold back His Son, and allowed Him to suffer for me?

My resolution:

Catechism Clip

CCC 314 We firmly believe that God is master of the world and of its history. But the ways of His providence are often unknown to us. Only at the end, when our partial knowledge ceases, when we see God "face to face" (1 Corinthians 13:12), will we fully know the ways by which—even through the dramas of evil and sin—God has guided His creation to that definitive Sabbath rest for which He created heaven and earth.

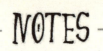

NOTES

Lesson 5

WELCOMED HOME ~ RECEIVING FORGIVENESS

Introduction

Have you ever felt that you just weren't good enough for God to love you? When you consider what you've done in the past, do you find you've made mistakes—big mistakes—that you think are too big for God to forgive? Do you think you have to have it all together in order to be acceptable to God?

I remember spending an afternoon with a dear friend who was recovering from a nervous breakdown. She had never wanted to talk with me about spiritual things before, so I was very surprised when she began to ask me about my faith. I talked to her about the many things God wants to give us: unconditional love, forgiveness, strength in our times of weakness. She listened, wistfully. "That's what He does for you," she said. "You haven't done the things I've done." Regardless of what I said, she felt she had surpassed the limits of Christ's forgiveness, and that her weaknesses and failures had disqualified her from receiving His blessings.

How different all our lives would be if we truly understood the heart of our heavenly Father. He longs for an intimate relationship with each one of us. He wants to blanket us with His grace and draw us in close. But all too often, we stand outside the door. Perhaps we feel disqualified. Perhaps we feel underdressed—naked, even—when we think about the fact that He knows everything there is to know about us. We wonder if a "close-up shot" of our shortcomings will cause Him to reject us.

God knows this. He knows what holds us back. So He tells us stories. He comes through the back door and catches us off guard by drawing us into a parable. It's only later that we realize the parable was actually *our story*.

We'll spend this whole lesson on parables that you are probably familiar with. You've likely heard this story before. But this time, let's ask God to help us hear His words in a fresh, new way. Let's turn down the volume of the voices that tell us, "You're not good enough. You've crossed the line. When you made that mistake, you went too far." Let's let Jesus speak for Himself.

Day One
SETTING THE STAGE

Read Luke 15:1–10.

1. While both tax collectors and Pharisees drew near to listen to Jesus, to whom did Jesus address these parables? See verses 1–3.

2. What had upset the Pharisees in verse 2?

To sit down and eat with someone had real significance during Jesus' day. It was more than just sharing a picnic bench. It symbolized acceptance and friendship. When Jesus behaved in this way, it flew in the face of the rules of "separation" and "purity" that the Pharisees followed.

3. What is the common theme in each of the three parables of Luke 15?

4. How do you think Jesus' words in verses 7 and 10 made the Pharisees feel?

Welcomed Home ~ Receiving Forgiveness | 5

Quiet your heart and enjoy His presence. . . . Jesus invites "the poor and the crippled, the blind and the lame" (Luke 14:21).

The way that the Pharisees responded to "sinners" contrasted sharply with Jesus' approach. The Pharisees' message? You are condemned and past the reach of God's mercy. Jesus' message? Come and sit with me—you are welcome at my table.

Some of us have encountered Pharisees on our faith journey, and some of us have acted like them. All of us are in equal need of God's mercy and grace. This will be the focus of our lesson, and I pray it draws us all in equal measure to an awareness of our need for forgiveness.

Take a few moments to ask the Lord to remove any blindness that is keeping you from seeing your need of a savior. He wants to help us see our need for Him if we are making poor moral choices, and just as much if we're steeped in self-righteousness. No matter which category we tend toward, He invites us to sit at the table and draw near.

Day Two
THE YOUNGER SON

Read Luke 15:11–32.

1. What was the younger son communicating to his father when he asked for his share of his father's estate? Note: At that time, when a father died, the oldest child received double the amount that younger siblings inherited. In a family with two sons, the oldest would receive two-thirds of all that the father had, and the younger son would receive one-third. But this would only occur when the father was dead.

One would expect that the father would be offended by this request, but instead, he did what his son asked. The property was divided and given to both his sons.

2. What was the son willing to do in order to earn his way when he returned home?

3. After the younger son received his inheritance, he went to a distant country and squandered it. Feeling hungry and needy, he decided to return home. His father had every right to refuse to receive him back; the son had paid him the ultimate disrespect. How did the father receive his younger son?

4. What was the significance of the father's actions? He was communicating that his son *was not going to have to earn his way back into his favor.* The father welcomed his son with grace—utterly undeserved favor. This is the way that God welcomes us into His family, too. When we turn toward Him and ask if we can come home, He opens His arms wide. He covers our nakedness with His robe of righteousness. We don't earn that place—it's a free gift. Does this parable challenge the way you have previously thought about how your heavenly Father receives you?

Quiet your heart and enjoy His presence. . . . There are no limits to Christ's forgiveness.

If you are coming up with reasons why what you have done is worse than what the younger son did, stop right now. You are not the exception to this rule. God's grace is more than enough to cover anything that you have done. He offers you His forgiveness and beckons you home. He wants you. He longs for you. Can you picture a runner at the beginning of a race, poised and ready for the gun to go off? That's God, poised and ready to come rushing toward you, ready to pounce on you with love and extravagant grace and limitless mercy. But He waits, because He will not force Himself on you. He is a gentleman. Are you ready to come home?

Day Three
THE OLDER SON

When we read the parable of the Prodigal Son, we can be left with the impression that the grace freely given to the younger son didn't have a cost. The truth is, it didn't cost the younger son anything. It didn't actually cost the father, either. Who paid the price? It was the older son.

The father had given all he had to his two sons. In reinstating the younger son, he was asking the older son to share what he had inherited with his wild-child, undeserving little brother.

Reread Luke 15:23–32, putting yourself in the shoes of the elder brother.

1. What was the first emotion the older son had when he heard how his brother was being welcomed? Why did he feel this way? What would an alternative (better) reaction have been? See verse 28.

2. What did the father do when his older son refused to come in? See verse 28.

3. What reason did the older son give for not coming in? See verse 29.

When we look more intently at this story, we see that the two brothers weren't as different as they first appeared. Both of them wanted something from their father. The younger decided to just reach out and grab it. The older felt a better method would be to always follow the rules, so that in the end, he would deserve everything he got. Neither loved the father just for himself. They wanted *what he gave* more than they wanted *him*. Rebellion divided the younger son from his father. Pride divided the older son from his father. Both sons used the father to get what they wanted. Both were in need of forgiveness.

Quiet your heart and enjoy His presence. . . . He invites you to come home. When we put the three parables of Luke 15 (the lost sheep, lost coin, and lost son) into context and remember that Jesus was talking to the Pharisees, we are forced to broaden our interpretation of the stories. In the words of theologian Tim Keller, "Jesus is pleading not so much with immoral outsiders as with moral insiders."[24] Moral insiders are the rule keepers. When their behavior is held up to the Ten Commandments, they come out looking shiny and good. But clearly, Jesus is concerned about more than outward behavior.

Through these parables, Jesus redefined what it means to be lost. It wasn't just the sheep, the coin, and the younger brother who needed to be found. The elder brother, the rule keeper, was in equal need of forgiveness.

How can you tell if you're more like the older son? Take some time to prayerfully think about how you feel when things don't go your way. Do you get angry because you feel like you deserve things to go well since you are working so hard to obey God? Deep down, do you feel like God should bless you because of the way that you serve Him? Are you trying to control your life through your performance?

The older son obeyed his father to get what he wanted. Why do you obey?

Christ's forgiveness is limitless. The only prerequisite is knowing that you need it.

Day Four
SHEER GRATUITOUS LOVE

1. In the parables of Luke 15, the shepherd didn't stop seeking until he found the one missing sheep, the woman didn't rest until she found her one missing coin, and the father watched the road, waiting hopefully for his son's return. What insight do these parables give into the very personal love God has for each of us?

2. Read CCC 218, 219, and 220. What insight do you gain from the Catechism clips regarding God's forgiveness?

---

[24] Timothy Keller, *The Prodigal God* (New York: Penguin Group, 2008), 10.

3. The only thing that can limit Christ's forgiveness is our refusal to ask for it. This is why it's so critical that we recognize whether we are more like the younger or the older son. Typically, the "younger son" knows that what he is doing is wrong. He knows he needs forgiveness. The older son, though, can be easily blinded by self-righteousness. We don't need forgiveness just for the bad things we've done. We also need to ask forgiveness for the good things we've done for the wrong reasons. If we do good things in order to earn our salvation, we have put ourselves in Jesus' place. We have made the decision (consciously or not) to be our own savior. We have gotten so busy trying to save ourselves that we have lost sight of our need for rescue. Allow the following questions to sink deep into your heart. Take the time to answer them truthfully. At the end of this reflection, you may feel a need to confess that your self-dependence has kept you from dependence on God. Don't ignore this call from the Holy Spirit. Don't put it off. The time to bring this before the Lord is now. He is waiting for you—He is the father standing in the road, ready to run and blanket you in forgiveness and mercy.

Are you trying to control your life through your performance?

Do you feel that obeying God should result in a smoother road ahead?

Are you motivated to obey God out of a fear of punishment, or out of love for Him?

Do you think you might be trying to earn God's love and salvation?

What is prayer for you? Is it a way to increase the likelihood of getting what you want or is it a time of intimacy with your friend?

Quiet your heart and enjoy His presence. . . . He is longing for you.

How I pray that reflecting on those questions hasn't caused anyone to feel condemned. I know that's a risk. Part of it is because we are so hard on ourselves. We want so badly to get it right, and when we realize that we've been doing something good for the wrong reasons, our anger can turn inward. "How could I? What's wrong with me? Why can't I ever get it right?" Please hear me on this: That voice of condemnation does not come from Jesus. "There is no condemnation for those who are in Christ Jesus" (Romans 8:1). The Holy Spirit convicts us (this is different from condemning us) in order to draw us into a good, healthy, holy relationship with God. He wants to lead you to a place where you obey God out of love for Him—not out of fear of getting punished. God wants to be wanted for Himself, not for the things He gives. He offers you the gift of limitless forgiveness so that anything between your heart and His can be cleared away. He loves you so very, very much.

Day Five
SAINT'S STORY

Saint Maria Goretti

Where Saint Maria Goretti grew up, anger was in the very air she breathed, mixed with the malaria that claimed one life after another. Her family was her refuge, a circle of peace and love in difficult times.

She was born into poverty, but after her father died of malaria, their poverty became misery. Maria's mother had to give up the farm and find work in the service of other farmers, so they moved to the marshlands outside Nettuno, Italy. There, her mother worked the fields while Maria sewed and cared for the little ones.

The Gorettis shared a small house with another farm worker, Giovanni Serenelli, and his twenty-year-old son, Alessandro. Giovanni tried to drown his anger in drink, and Maria and her mother would be terrorized as he'd enter the building drunk, cursing and banging into the walls and doors and throwing things.

But it was Alessandro she feared the most. If Giovanni flared up in hot anger, Alessandro nursed a cold anger that ran deeper, corrupting his heart. The anger inside him was like a shadow that darkened and chilled the room when he was home, sucking away all of the oxygen.

Welcomed Home ~ Receiving Forgiveness | 5

No doubt, it was the anger inside Alessandro that made him do what he did—anger and hatred, resentment for the misery of his life ankle-deep in marshland mud, fury at the hopelessness of his future, and frustration at having dreams and desires unmet. He had already cornered Maria and tried to rape her twice before, and she had escaped like a bird from the fowler's snare. But he had threatened to kill her if she told anyone of his failed attempts, so she kept quiet. As a wolf seizes its prey by the neck to silence it, so Alessandro silenced her.

Maria was doing her needlework in the house and watching over her sleeping infant sister when the door banged open and she saw Alessandro's shadow in the doorway. A wave of hatred and anger swept into the room with him and a prayer rose up in her throat.

It all happened so quickly. He forced himself on her; she fought him off. She tried to reason with him: "Alessandro, it is a mortal sin! If you do this, you will go to hell!" She tried to save him and herself. But something inside him broke and all that latent fury was unleashed on twelve-year-old Maria. He swung an ice pick again and again into her small frame, ten inches of metal plunging into her chest, throat, and heart. He stabbed her eleven times. Bathed in blood, she tried to crawl to the door, which only enraged him more. He lunged at her, stabbed her three more times, and then ran away.

The baby woke up and began to cry. Maria entrusted herself to God and the Blessed Virgin Mary, prayed to be found, prayed for Alessandro, prayed for her mother, and prayed for God to accept her soul. Her flesh was ravaged, with fourteen stab wounds gushing blood. But her heart was at peace. It was not only her virginity that was spared that day. It was also the purity of her heart, which even then chose not to hate. By the grace of God, she chose to forgive.

It is always a choice to forgive. It is a question not of emotions, but of the heart, that deepest center where we decide who we want to be, how we want to live, and how we want to die. Jesus shows us the way; it is our choice to walk it.

Forgiveness is also an act of faith. Even when her body was in the hands of her enemy, Maria trusted that her heart and her soul were safe in the hands of God, and that there was no snatching away from Him. She trusted that no matter what happened, her Good Shepherd would never abandon her.

Yes, she walked through the marshes and the misery, touching the anger and the hopelessness all around her. But that malaria of resentment did not infect her; she did not let it in. She kept her soul virgin, free of vengeance, nourished with grace and love, like a lamb grazing in fields of green.

After her death, Maria Goretti appeared to Alessandro in a dream, bearing fourteen white lilies in her arms. He had walled himself off from everyone for three years, refusing to communicate, unrepentant, locked in the interior prison of his own anger, unable to forgive himself. She presented him with the white lilies—her pardon—and when he reached out to take them, they turned into flames that burned his hands. She told him that it was time to let go of the anger that burned inside him, making his soul a blackened wasteland, sterile and hard. It was time to let forgiveness wash through him like a river, time to let God turn his desert into green, healthy land. It was time to be made new.

Alessandro listened, by a special grace. He turned and was healed. In accepting her forgiveness, he also learned to forgive; he learned to let go of the darkness he had been clinging to so tightly.

Are we not all a little like Alessandro? It is pride that makes us cling to our anger. Perhaps we were wronged; perhaps our life was changed, derailed, or even destroyed by the actions of another who remains unrepentant and indifferent to our fate. Perhaps we have many reasons to cherish a secret rage or a lingering resentment. Perhaps the one we find it hardest to forgive is ourselves. And in response to the hurt we have suffered, we want to inflict it in return.

But we are the ones who suffer most from unforgiveness. Why not let go and trust God to heal the wounds that you carry? He can make lilies grow where bleeding holes were. He can turn a tragedy into a path of growth. But He cannot do it unless we open the door and let His forgiveness become our forgiveness. Once we do, God alone knows what miracles He can work.

Alessandro and Maria's mother were reconciled and he eventually became a lay brother with the Order of Friars Minor Capuchin, where he worked as a receptionist, welcoming people in, and a gardener, making green things grow. Alessandro was healed. And twenty years after witnessing Saint Maria Goretti's canonization in 1950, he died of old age, in peace. He had come a long way from the malaria fields to the Good Shepherd's fold.

Forgiveness is a powerful thing.

In what area of your life would you like to experience the power of forgiveness? Is there someone you need to forgive? Is that person yourself? Or is God stirring your heart to ask someone to forgive you?

Conclusion

It's a sobering thought to realize that both sons—the rule-bending youngest and the rule-following eldest—were in equal need of forgiveness. The cross is the great equalizer. We *all* require the mercy that flows from Jesus' sacrifice.

Those of us who recognize ourselves in the older son will struggle with this concept. It doesn't feel right. The sense that we somehow deserve our salvation because we've followed the rules can get rooted pretty deeply in our hearts. The only thing that will pull it out is a deeper understanding of the gospel.

Forgiveness always comes at a cost. In the case of the Prodigal Son, the price was paid by the older son. What about in our case? Is there a cost to our forgiveness? Who paid the price for you and me?

It was a firstborn son who came to our aid. But He didn't sit at home, waiting to see if we'd stop wandering and start the journey back home. He stepped off His throne and came looking for us. When He found us, He didn't just share His inheritance. It cost Him *everything* to bring us home and welcome us back into the family. Even though we were dirty and poor, Jesus was not (and is not) ashamed to call us brothers and sisters (Hebrews 2:11).

Just as the father stood outside the feast and begged his oldest son to come in, God issues an invitation to each of us. He has prepared a banquet and it waits for us in heaven. All those who have received the forgiveness He offers will be welcome at the table.

What will the feast be like? The Old Testament prophet Isaiah described it as "a feast of rich food and choice wines, juicy, rich food and pure, choice wines. On this mountain he will destroy the veil that veils all peoples, the web that is woven over all nations. He will destroy death forever. The Lord God will wipe away the tears from all faces; the reproach of his people he will remove from the whole earth" (Isaiah 25:6–8).

That sounds like my kind of party.

Actually, to call it a party is rather an understatement. We read in the book of Revelation that it's going to be a *wedding feast*. Jesus, the Lamb of God, is the bridegroom, and we are the bride.

> "Let us rejoice and be glad and give him glory! For the wedding day of the Lamb has come, his bride has made herself ready. She was allowed to wear a bright, clean linen garment." (The linen represents the righteous deeds of the holy ones.) Then the angel said to me, "Write this: Blessed are those who have been called to the wedding feast of the Lamb." And he said to me, "These words are true; they come from God." . . . Then I saw the heavens opened, and there was a white horse; its rider was called "Faithful and True." . . . He has a name written on his cloak and on his thigh, "King of kings and Lord of lords." (Revelation 19:7–9, 11, 16)

We have been called to the wedding feast of the Lamb. These are the days when we (the bride) are making ourselves ready. Limitless, freely offered forgiveness will wash us clean and allow us to be presented to our groom with radiance and purity. Let's get ready to feast.

My Resolution

In what specific way will I apply what I have learned in this lesson?

Examples:

1. In order to remind myself of God's love for me, I will read Romans 8:38–39 each morning: "For I am convinced that neither death, nor life, nor angels, nor principalities, nor present things, nor future things, nor powers, nor height nor depth, nor any other creature will be able to separate us from the love of God in Christ Jesus our Lord."

2. If I am struggling to believe that God can really forgive all my sins, I will memorize 1 John 1:9: "If we acknowledge our sins, he is faithful and just and will forgive our sins and cleanse us from every wrongdoing."

3. I'll begin each day by spending five minutes thinking about what it cost Jesus to have me welcomed to the family and invited to the wedding supper of the Lamb. I'll thank Him for being willing to come out and find me when I was lost.

4. If I struggle in the same areas as the older son (in the parable of the Prodigal Son), I will check my heart each day for anger. Am I angry with God because things didn't go my way? Am I angry with myself for not being perfect? I'll ask God for forgiveness if I discover anger in my heart.

My resolution:

Catechism Clips

CCC 218 In the course of its history, Israel was able to discover that God had only one reason to reveal Himself to them, a single motive for choosing them from among all peoples as His special possession: His sheer gratuitous love. And thanks to the prophets, Israel understood that it was again out of love that God never stopped saving them and pardoning their unfaithfulness and sins.

CCC 219 God's love for Israel is compared to a father's love for his son. His love for His people is stronger than a mother's love for her children. God loves His people more than a bridegroom his beloved; His love will be victorious over even the worst infidelities, and it extends to His most precious gift: "God so loved the world that he gave his only Son" (John 3:16).

CCC 220 God's love is "everlasting" (Isaiah 54:8): "For the mountains may depart and the hills be removed, but my steadfast love shall not depart from you" (Isaiah 54:10). Through Jeremiah, God declares to his people, "I have loved you with an everlasting love; therefore I have continued my faithfulness to you" (Jeremiah 31:3).

NOTES

Walking with Purpose is a community of women growing in faith – together! This is where women are gathering. Join us!

www.walkingwithpurpose.com/find-program-near

Lesson 6

EMPOWERED ~ READING THE BIBLE

Introduction

As we come to the end of *Steadfast* and the *Opening Your Heart* series, you may be wondering how you can keep reading the Bible in a meaningful way on your own. You've seen the difference it makes to spend time with God in the pages of Scripture. But what should you do without the help of the guided questions in this study? You want to keep growing spiritually, but perhaps you could use some tips on how to structure time alone with Jesus. This lesson will focus on the how-to of spending quality time with the lover of your soul.

It may make you nervous to think of opening up the Bible on your own without a study guide alongside. You may be wondering if you're allowed to approach Scripture in this way or if this is something reserved for the clergy or people with theology degrees. If that's where you're at, you can rest assured knowing that the Catechism teaches us that "The Church forcefully and specifically exhorts all the Christian faithful . . . to learn 'the surpassing knowledge of Jesus Christ,' by frequent reading of the divine Scriptures" (CCC 133).

That being said, the Second Vatican Council gave three criteria for interpreting Scripture. These guidelines aren't given to discourage us from opening up the Bible on our own. They are meant to prevent us from setting ourselves up as the supreme authority, wrongly drawing conclusions from the Bible that God never intended. We find the three criteria in CCC 112–114. Here's a summary:

CCC 112 *"Be especially attentive 'to the content and unity of the whole Scripture.'"*
In other words, interpret Scripture in light of the overall message of the Bible—the story of God's plan of salvation. Don't take verses out of context. Pay attention to the literary form that's being used. Is it poetry? A letter of instruction? Prophecy? Historical narrative? Knowing what kind of writing it is will help you read it in the way it is meant to be read.

CCC 113 *"Read the Scripture within 'the living Tradition of the whole Church." According to a saying of the Fathers, Sacred Scripture is written principally in the Church's heart rather than in documents and records, for the Church carries in her Tradition the living memorial of God's Word."*

Because the Catholic Church existed before the entire Bible was penned, we believe in the importance of the oral teaching that has been passed down to us. As Catholics, we have at our disposal the teaching of the early Church fathers and the magisterium. (The early Church fathers were the earliest teachers in the Church. The magisterium is the teaching office of the Church, made up of the pope and the bishops, and it lays out what is the authentic teaching of the Church.) Our interpretation of Scripture should not conflict with those teachings.

CCC 114 *"Be attentive to the analogy of faith."*
This means that when we encounter a difficult text, the teachings of tradition and the analogy of faith lead the way. Analogy of faith is "the Catholic doctrine that every individual statement of belief must be understood in the light of the Church's whole objective body of faith."[25]

As we read the Bible, we need to remember that while it is God's love letter to us, it is primarily about Him. We are in the story, but it is *His* story. This means that we should ask, "What does this mean?" before we ask, "What does this mean to me?" We must seek to understand what a passage meant *then* (in context) before determining what it means *now*. Some parts of the Bible won't make sense if we read them thinking it's all about us instead of looking at the big picture of God's overarching plan of redemption for mankind.

But we don't just approach Scripture intellectually. We approach God's Word with our emotions, too. God wants *all of us*. He looks at each one of us as a whole. He doesn't just want to engage our minds—He cares deeply about the state of our hearts. Because of this, we can come to Scripture with our emotions in a hot mess, praying that God will guide us to a better place. In the words of Bible teacher Hayley Morgan, "We approach Scripture emotionally—that we would be restored to God's best way of handling those emotions." In doing so, we bring our humanity under God's authority, and ask Him to refine our humanness. We go to His Word saying, "Relieve the troubles of my heart, bring me out of my distress" (Psalm 25:17).

Pick up your Bible. You hold in your hands the story of God's relentless love for you. It's a love story about the Prince of Peace, who came to rescue you, His bride. It's a story about your spiritual family, your heritage. The whole lot of us have been up and

---

[25] John A. Hardon, *Modern Catholic Dictionary* (Bardstown, KY: Eternal Life, 2000).

down in our faithfulness to God. But God has always remained steady. He's never wavered in His love for a single person in the Bible, or a single one of His children who came afterward. God waits to speak to your heart every day. Don't let a single one pass by without hearing His voice.

Day One
GETTING STARTED

This week, you'll need your Bible and a prayer journal. I'm giving you an excuse to go shopping. You're welcome. You won't actually need the journal until tomorrow, but I thought you might like to give it some time so you can choose one that's really fabulous.

1. Although you can pray and read the Bible at any time of the day, what special benefits might there be in spending quality time with Jesus in the morning? See Psalm 90:14 and Mark 1:35.

If we're going to spend time alone with Jesus, we've got to come up with a time and a place when we can be by ourselves. We all love sleep. Getting up earlier in order to spend time with God can seem like a tall order. But could you start small? Could you give up just ten minutes of sleep so that your first thoughts could be of God?

You may be in a season of life when it feels impossible to get up even ten minutes earlier. If that's the case, I encourage you to look for the first pocket of quiet in your day, and reserve it for God. At some point, a pocket of quiet will come. What will you do with it? Check e-mails? Catch up on social media? Run an errand? Or open your Bible? The choice is yours.

2. Regardless of what time of day you decide to meet with God, I encourage you to consider it an appointment. Put it on your calendar, and then honor it just as you would any other commitment.

The best time for my appointment with God is:

The best place for my appointment with God is:

What are some external obstacles I need to overcome to stay committed to the best time and place in order to concentrate well?

3. Why should you always begin your time with God by inviting the Holy Spirit to come and be your teacher? See John 16:13–14 and 2 Peter 1:20–21.

Quiet your heart and enjoy His presence. . . . Meet Him early, and begin with prayer.

Take a moment to think about this mind-blowing truth: The maker of the universe is with you. He's listening to you.

Begin your time with the Lord with a simple prayer like Psalm 119:18: "Open my eyes to see clearly the wonders of your law." Invite the Holy Spirit to be your teacher. Ask Him to convict you of anything that needs to change, to comfort you when your heart is aching, and to direct you when you feel confused.

Day Two
PREPARING YOUR HEART

When God looks at you, He looks at you as a whole. He considers your heart (your emotions, dreams, desires, fears, hurts, etc.) to be an integral part of who you are. He longs to see you experience interior freedom and peace.

We read in Luke 6:45 that "out of the overflow of the heart the mouth speaks." This means that whatever is deep in our hearts will eventually come out. The safest place to explore our feelings is in the presence of God.

Beginning your time with God by prayer journaling allows you to bring your emotions to Him, inviting Him to help you sort through them all. It helps identify where you need forgiveness, healing, and guidance. This is different from self-focused navel-gazing because while you are sorting through what's in your heart, you are keeping your focus on God.

There's no "right" way to journal your prayers. The following format is provided as a springboard, a loose guide—a starting point.

1. I'm especially grateful to you, God, for these three things:

2. Instead of racing through life, I want to be fully present in the moment. This is when I've felt the most soul-satisfied recently:

3. Lord, I know you created me with a specific purpose in mind. I want my life to have meaning. I don't want to miss your plan for me. This is something I'm dreaming of right now:

4. God, please free me from the following fear:

5. Please forgive me for the following way in which I have failed to love you:

6. Recently, I noticed your glory in the following way:

7. Mother Mary, please mother me in this specific way:

Quiet your heart and enjoy His presence. . . . Come before Him wholeheartedly, holding nothing back.

"To you O Lord I lift up my soul, my God, in you I trust." (Psalm 25:1–2)

When you think about it, it's a little silly that we think we can hide our emotions from God. He sees everything, into the very depths of who we are. All the things we manage to conceal from people around us are totally visible to Him. And guess what? What He sees doesn't make Him run away. When He looks within each one of us, He actually draws closer in love. So we don't need to worry about presenting some cleaned-up version of ourselves to Him. We can be real. Reverent, because there's no one greater, but real because we are His beloved daughters, and He says, "Come as you are."

Day Three
THE DEVOTIONAL METHOD OF BIBLE STUDY EXPLAINED

Once you have prepared your heart to listen to God speak through the Scriptures, it's time to dive in! But where do you begin? This section of the lesson will show you how to prayerfully think about a passage of the Bible. The purpose of this method of study is to form a practical application from what you have read. As you read, you'll ask yourself the question, "What am I going to do with what I've learned?"

There are a number of different ways to read the Bible devotionally. You can use just one, or if you have more time, you can do them all. As is the case with everything, the more you put into it, the more you'll get out of it. You can record your study notes in the same journal you used for Day Two.

Ways to Read the Bible Devotionally:

1. <u>Place Yourself in the Scene</u>
   Picture yourself in the midst of the biblical scene. What would you have felt? What would you have done? Think about the historical context of the story. How would that change what you would have experienced if you were actually there? This way of meditating on a passage can make the people come alive to you.

2. Word Emphasis
   Read a Bible verse multiple times, and each time, emphasize a different word. Each emphasis will give a new meaning. For example, 2 Corinthians 5:17 could be read in this way:

   "**If** anyone is in Christ, he is a new creation."
   "If **anyone** is in Christ, he is a new creation."
   "If anyone **is** in Christ, he is a new creation."
   "If anyone is **in** Christ, he is a new creation."
   "If anyone is in **Christ**, he is a new creation."
   "If anyone is in Christ, **he** is a new creation."
   "If anyone is in Christ, he **is** a new creation."
   "If anyone is in Christ, he is a **new** creation."
   "If anyone is in Christ, he is a new **creation**."

3. Paraphrase the Bible Passage
   This means that you take the Bible passage and put it into your own words. When you summarize what you've read in this way, the core lesson often comes to the surface.

4. Personalize the Bible Passage
   You can personalize Scripture by putting your name in place of certain nouns and pronouns in the Bible passage. For example, in 1 Corinthians 13:4–7, you can replace the word *love* with your name:

   "_____ is patient, _____is kind. She is not jealous, she is not pompous, she is not inflated. _____ is not rude, she does not seek her own interests, she is not quick-tempered, she does not brood over injury. _____ does not rejoice over wrongdoing, but rejoices with the truth. _____bears all things, believes all things, hopes all things, endures all things." (Hmm . . . it's rather convicting.)

The final step after studying this passage is the most important. Ask yourself, "Now what am I supposed to do with this information? How can it help me to live more like Christ?" You can use this simple acrostic to tease out a personal application from the passage:

Is there a(n) . . .
Promise to claim?
Example to follow?
Attitude to change?
Command to obey?
Error to avoid?

Write your application down in your journal, and end your time with the Lord by prayerfully responding to what you have studied. The passage may lead you in prayer to praise, confess, or commit to a new path.

To reflect on why it's important to read and *apply* the Bible (this is what the devotional method does), record your thoughts on the following verses.

A. Matthew 7:24–27

B. James 4:17

C. 1 Corinthians 8:1

Quiet your heart and enjoy His presence. . . . Let the Holy Spirit guide you toward transformation.

Just knowing a lot about the Bible doesn't necessarily translate into the kind of transformed life that pleases God. The Sadducees were the priestly aristocracy, well versed in the Scriptures. They were the conservatives of the day, and highly esteemed the written law. Yet when Jesus spoke to them, He said, "You are misled because you do not know the scriptures or the power of God" (Matthew 22:29). They knew the Scriptures intellectually, but failed to apply the overall message. Their long-awaited Messiah, the source of salvation, stood right in front of them. For all their academic knowledge, they failed to recognize the truth.

Dear Lord,

I pray that you will never say to me what you said to the Sadducees: "You are misled because you do not know the scriptures or the power of God." I want to know both! Help me to live out James 1:22, to "be [a] doer of the word and not [a] hearer only, deluding [myself]."

Day Four
GIVE IT A TRY!

Let's dive in and give this a whirl. *You can do this*, and you'll feel so empowered when you realize that truly all you need is your Bible, a journal, and a teachable heart.

Be sure to start by preparing your heart with prayer (remember Day Two). Then choose the passage you'd like to study. Here are some suggestions:

Psalm 139 (my favorite psalm to read if I feel lonely or insignificant)

Isaiah 43:1–7 (powerful verses for when you feel overwhelmed; let these truths sink in *deep*)

Luke 1:46–55 (This is the "Magnificat," Mary's hymn of praise to the Lord; I love it. It's very interesting to think about what the Blessed Mother was feeling when she prayed these words.)

John 3:16–21 (when you need truth that's good and solid)

Philippians 4:4–8 (great when an attitude adjustment is needed)

James 1:19–27 (or maybe even a portion of this passage—it's so loaded with things that convict my heart, lots of times an application jumps out at me after just one verse)

Revelation 2:2–5 (Read this when you need a kick in the pants. Because sometimes we do. This is a great one to reflect on when you know that something has been competing for Jesus' place in your heart.)

Revelation 21:3–7 (when you need hope)

My Bible passage for today:

My study notes:
(Place yourself in the scene, emphasize certain words, paraphrase the passage, and personalize it.)

My application:

Quiet your heart and enjoy His presence. . . . Just you and the Lord. You're making Him so happy right now.

When we open up the Bible and ask the Holy Spirit to teach us, the Lord is absolutely thrilled. When we take the next step and obey what He's pointed out to us, He feels loved. Obedience is His love language.

This is where the rubber meets the road. What do we do with all we've learned? The Holy Spirit is working on us from within, giving us the desire and the power to change. But our part is to step out and be doers of the Word.

Not always, but often, that means doing the opposite of what we feel like. That's when our love is the most pure, because it's sacrificial. But be assured, not one little sacrifice goes unnoticed by the Lord. He sees. He remembers.

Dear Lord,

In John 15:5, you said, "I am the vine, you are the branches. He who abides in me, and I in him, he it is that bears much fruit, for apart from me you can do nothing." Someone was once asked how to spell abide *with four letters. The reply? O-B-E-Y. So I ask for your help in this. Obedience isn't easy. But I claim your promise in Philippians 4:13: "I can do all things through Christ who strengthens me." Apart from you, there's not a lot I can do, but with you, there's no limit to how sacrificial my love can be.*

Day Five
SAINT'S STORY

Saint Edith Stein

Saint Edith Stein's story is unusual. Born a Jew, she lived her youth as an atheist, worked as a philosopher, converted to the Catholic faith, and was martyred as a Carmelite nun in the gas chamber at Auschwitz in 1942.

Saint Edith Stein wasn't born a saint. Known to be iron-willed and headstrong, she went through a period of radical feminism and spent many years as an atheist. She struggled through a period of depression in her youth, and at the age of fourteen, she consciously and freely decided to give up praying and stopped practicing her Jewish religion. Instead, she immersed herself in study, pursuing truth through philosophy.

It took many years, but by the mercy of God, this profound thirst for truth led her back to Him in a deeper way. As she began to pore over the words of the New Testament, her heart was called home to the Catholic Church through its words.

Every soul hears the song of another homeland deep in the heart. Ultimately, we all yearn for heaven. Whether we realize it or not, we all thirst to see the face of Christ. Reading Scripture is one of the ways we can quench our "homesickness." It gives us a reminder of God's sovereignty—that He has always had a plan and continues to be the supreme authority over all, even when it seems like everything is out of control. Through its pages, we hear His voice of love, comfort, and strength.

When Edith was a laywoman living in the world, already Catholic, she used to go by herself to a chapel in the city where she worked. There, she would kneel before the tabernacle for hours at a time. She would close her eyes and go deep inside her heart and soul. Sometimes she would say nothing at all. It was an experience of deep stillness in God, of silence, and of letting go and offering herself over and over again without words.

What resulted from Saint Edith Stein's deep devotional life was a total surrender of her heart. She let herself be filled with His will like an empty vessel is filled with the choicest ointments. And when the time came for the vessel to be broken, the perfume of her surrender filled the Church and the world with its fragrance.

Don't assume that such obedience is beyond you. It is always within reach, because every surrender is a work of the Holy Spirit within us. It is God Himself within you who knits your heart to Christ and strengthens His life within you. You pray in your words; He prays in His with "unspeakable groanings," as Saint Paul says in Romans 8:26.

When you prayerfully read Scripture, Jesus is able to enter your life in a deeper way, healing wounds that you didn't even know you had. He enters your soul with gentleness and understanding, working silently while you think nothing is happening. He enlarges your capacity to love and adorns you with grace.

That is why we must never judge our prayers or get discouraged, thinking, "I can't pray. I can't read the Bible. I don't feel anything. Nothing is happening." This is not for us to judge. Must the canvas understand everything the Divine Artist is painting? Perhaps some brushstrokes are so light that they escape notice. And yet, those details may be the most beautiful of all.

The spiritual life is a relationship between a lover and His beloved. It is not a personal resolution for self-perfection or a business contract. It is a friendship full of trust and affection, a bond of love that deepens into the ultimate gift of self. This is what your time reading the Bible can become: a conversation that draws you ever deeper into the heart of Christ.

And when the time comes for your soul to return to its maker, you will find that death is nothing to be feared. Because you have prayed and touched the face of Christ in darkness, the unveiling will be an occasion of great joy.

And when you do see His face, you will realize that you have finally come home.

Can you find ideas in the spiritual life of Saint Edith Stein that can enliven your own?

Conclusion

"And we, who with unveiled faces all reflect the Lord's glory, are being transformed into his likeness with ever-increasing glory, which comes from the Lord, who is the Spirit." (2 Corinthians 3:18)

Unveiled faces reflecting God's glory.

These words make me think of a woman making sure that nothing is getting between her and her God. She holds out her heart to Him, just as it is. She comes into His presence, full of emotions and needs, and asks Him to sort it all out. And He does.

And she is utterly transformed, from the inside out. As a result, she reflects Him to a world in desperate need of His touch.

Everywhere she goes, she spreads "the fragrance of the knowledge of him . . . [she is] the aroma of Christ" (2 Corinthians 2:14–15). That aroma is described by She Reads Truth founder Amanda Williams in this way:

> *An aroma is something experienced.* It transforms the air simply because of what it is. **Sisters, we are the aroma of Christ.**
> Not peddlers of a way of life.
> Not salespeople for a system of beliefs.
> **We are those commissioned by God to transform the very air in which we live, not because of who we are but because of who He is . . .**
> It truly is all about Him. And what *He's* all about is love.
> Mercy. Grace. Wholeness. Justice. Redemption. Hope. These are the things that should come from our steeping our souls in God's Word. We are not to wield it as a weapon to beat the unbelieving into submission. **We are simply to hold out Christ.**[26]

We've come to the end of our study, but it's only the beginning of a beautiful journey for you. Day by day, as you turn to God and spend time with Him in prayer and the Scriptures, you are being changed into His likeness. You are no longer defined by your past mistakes. A fresh path stretches before you. As you run toward Him, the old you is stripped away and you are changed. What remains is all that is *the best of you*. You bear the image of God, and the more you are with Him, the more you become like Him.

This is my prayer for each one of us—that we would come before the Lord with unveiled faces, and then go out, giving everyone we meet a little glimpse of who He is.

My Resolution

In what specific way will I apply what I have learned in this lesson?

---

[26] Amanda Bible Williams, "It Is a Merciful Fragrance," She Reads Truth, March 4, 2014, http://shereadstruth.com/2014/03/04/merciful-fragrance/.

Examples:

1. I'll set up a spot where I'll spend time alone with God each day. It'll help me to diligently keep that appointment if I make sure all the things I need (Bible, journal, pen) are there.

2. I will set my alarm ten minutes early every day this week in order to spend time alone with God.

3. I'll ask a friend to hold me accountable for living out the personal application I find each day in my Bible reading.

My resolution:

Catechism Clips

The Second Vatican Council indicates three criteria for interpreting Scripture in accordance with the Spirit who inspired it.

CCC 112 *Be especially attentive "to the content and unity of the whole Scripture"*. Different as the books which compose it may be, Scripture is a unity by reason of the unity of God's plan, of which Christ Jesus is the center and heart, open since his Passover.

> The phrase "heart of Christ" can refer to Sacred Scripture, which makes known his heart, closed before the Passion, as the Scripture was obscure. But the Scripture has been opened since the Passion; since those who from then on have understood it, consider and discern in what way the prophecies must be interpreted.

CCC 113 *Read the Scripture within "the living Tradition of the whole Church"*. According to a saying of the Fathers, Sacred Scripture is written principally in the Church's heart rather than in documents and records, for the Church carries in her Tradition the living memorial of God's Word, and it is the Holy Spirit who gives her the spiritual interpretation of the Scripture ("... according to the spiritual meaning which the Spirit grants to the Church").

CCC 114 *Be attentive to the analogy of faith*. By "analogy of faith" we mean the coherence of the truths of faith among themselves and within the whole plan of Revelation.

NOTES

No program near you? No problem...it's easy to start your own group in your parish or at home and we will walk with you every step of the way. Find out more:

www.walkingwithpurpose.com/leadership

Appendices

Appendix 1
SAINT THÉRÈSE OF LISIEUX

Patron Saint of Walking with Purpose

Saint Thérèse of Lisieux was gifted with the ability to take the riches of our Catholic faith and explain them in a way that a child could imitate. The wisdom she gleaned from Scripture ignited a love in her heart for her Lord that was personal and transforming. The simplicity of the faith that she laid out in her writings is so completely Catholic that Pope Pius XII said, "She rediscovered the Gospel itself, the very heart of the Gospel."

Walking with Purpose is intended to be a means by which women can honestly share their spiritual struggles and embark on a journey that is refreshing to the soul. It was never intended to facilitate the deepest of intellectual study of Scripture. Instead, the focus has been to help women know Christ: to know His heart, to know His tenderness, to know His mercy, and to know His love. Our logo is a little flower, and that has meaning. When a woman begins to open her heart to God, it's like the opening of a little flower. It can easily be bruised or crushed, and it must be treated with the greatest of care. Our desire is to speak to women's hearts no matter where they are in life, baggage and all, and gently introduce truths that can change their lives.

Saint Thérèse of Lisieux, the little flower, called her doctrine "the little way of spiritual childhood," and it is based on complete and unshakable confidence in God's love for us. She was not introducing new truths. She spent countless hours reading Scripture and she shared what she found, emphasizing the importance of truths that had already been divinely revealed. We can learn so much from her:

> The good God would not inspire unattainable desires; I can, then, in spite of my littleness, aspire to sanctity. For me to become greater is impossible; I must put up with myself just as I am with all my imperfections. But I wish to find the way to go to Heaven by a very straight, short, completely new little way. We are in a century of inventions: now one does not even have to take the trouble to climb the steps of a stairway; in the homes of the rich, an elevator replaces them nicely. I, too, would like to find an elevator to lift me up to Jesus, for I

am too little to climb the rough stairway of perfection. So I have looked in the books of the saints for a sign of the elevator I long for, and I have read these words proceeding from the mouth of eternal Wisdom: "He that is a little one, let him turn to me" (Proverbs 9:16). So I came, knowing that I had found what I was seeking, and wanting to know, O my God, what You would do with the little one who would answer Your call, and this is what I found:

"As one whom the mother caresses, so will I comfort you. You shall be carried at the breasts and upon the knees they shall caress you" (Isaiah 66:12–13). Never have more tender words come to make my soul rejoice. The elevator which must raise me to the heavens is Your arms, O Jesus! For that I do not need to grow; on the contrary, I must necessarily remain small, become smaller and smaller. O my God, You have surpassed what I expected, and I want to sing Your mercies. (Saint Thérèse of the Infant Jesus, *Histoire d'une Ame: Manuscrits Autobiographiques* [Paris: Éditions du Seuil, 1998], 244.)

Answer Key

Answer Key

Lesson 1, Day One
1. **A.** Answers will vary.
   B. The psalmist saw the hand of God creating him, intentionally forming him into a wonderful, known person. He saw God caring about each detail of his life, shaping his days even before he was born. He considered himself wonderfully made—a one-of-a-kind work of art.
2. **A.** People judge based on appearance and status, but God is different. He looks deep within us—He looks at our hearts.
   B. Answers will vary.
3. **A.** Jesus did not save us because of righteous deeds we have done. He saved us because He is kind, generous, and merciful.
   B. He saved us through the bath of rebirth and renewal by the Holy Spirit (the sacrament of baptism), which was poured out on us. He saved us so that we could be justified by His grace and become heirs in hopes of eternal life.
   C. We were saved while we were still sinners.
4. **A.** Through faith and baptism, we are now children of God.
   B. God sent the Holy Spirit to live in us to prove that we are His children. We are to call God our Abba—our daddy.
5. We can be led by the Spirit of God. This is not a spirit that causes us to fall back into fear, but one of adoption, that allows us to cry, "Abba, Father!" The Holy Spirit testifies with our spirit that we are children of God.

Lesson 1, Day Two
1. **A.** Answers will vary.
   B. In this verse, Jesus tells us that it wasn't a matter of us choosing Him. *He* has chosen *us*. He wants us.
2. We are to guard our hearts.
3. **Song of Songs 4:7** "You are beautiful in every way, my friend, there is no flaw in you!"
   Isaiah 41:10 "Do not fear; I am with you; do not be anxious; I am your God. I will strengthen you, I will help you, I will uphold you with my victorious right hand."
   Isaiah 43:4 "Because you are precious in my eyes and honored, and I love you, I give people in return for you and nations in exchange for your life."
   Isaiah 49:15–16 "Can a mother forget her infant, be without tenderness for the child of her womb? Even should she forget, I will never forget you. See, upon the palms of my hands I have engraved you; your walls are ever before me."
   Psalm 34:8 "The angel of the Lord encamps around those who fear him, and he saves them."
   Psalm 56:9 "My wanderings you have noticed; are my tears not stored in your flask, recorded in your book?"
   Exodus 14:14 "The Lord will fight for you; you have only to keep still."
   1 Corinthians 1:27–29 "God chose the foolish of the world to shame the wise, and God chose the weak of the world to shame the strong, and God chose the lowly and despised of the world, those who count for nothing, to reduce to nothing those who are something, so that no human being might boast before God."
   John 14:1–3 "Do not let your hearts be troubled. You have faith in God; have faith also in me. In my Father's house there are many dwelling places. If there were not, would I have told you that I am going to prepare a place for you? And if I go and prepare a place for you, I will come back again and take you to myself, so that where I am you also may be."

Lesson 1, Day Three
1. **A.** These verses tell us to be on our guard, to stand firm in the faith, to be courageous, and to be strong.
   B. Answers will vary.
2. Answers will vary.
3. **A.** According to Philippians 3:20, our citizenship is in heaven.
   B. That community is described as a "great cloud of witnesses."
   C. The great cloud of witnesses is watching us run the race that lies before us.
   D. Answers will vary.

Lesson 1, Day Four
1. **A.** Jesus tells us that we aren't to worry about what we eat, drink, or wear. God knows what we need. We're told to seek *first* the kingdom of God and His righteousness, and then all the things we need will be given to us.
   B. Answers will vary.
2. Answers will vary.
3. **Matthew 6:24–25** Jesus said that if we are going to be His followers, we must deny ourselves and take up our cross. If we lose our life in the worldly sense, we'll actually gain it eternally.
   John 12:24-25 Just as a grain of wheat "dies" when it's buried in the ground, but then bears fruit, our little deaths, our sacrifices, produce fruit as well.
   Philippians 3:8 Saint Paul considered all earthly gains to be rubbish in comparison to the surpassing value of knowing Christ.
4. **A.** Answers will vary.
   B. Answers will vary.

Lesson 2, Day One
1. Peter took his eyes off of Jesus and focused on the waves. He was saved from drowning because Jesus reached out His hand and caught him.
2. He's given us a spirit of power, love, and self-control.
3. Answers will vary.

Lesson 2, Day Two
1. No. Jesus said that in this world we'll actually have trouble. But He encouraged us to take heart, because He has overcome the world.
2. She learned that everything passes; our troubles have an end date. Only God never changes. If we are patient in our difficulties, we'll learn that God alone is enough.
3. **A.** We don't walk alone. This passage encourages us to be strong and steadfast; to have no fear, for it is the Lord, our God, who marches with us; He will never fail us or forsake us.
   B. In Jesus' presence, we are never in darkness. He is our light and He promises to save us. Because He is with us, we don't need to be afraid.
   C. God is always with us. He promises to always strengthen and uphold us.
   D. Nothing can separate us from the love of God. Nothing.
4. Answers will vary.

Lesson 2, Day Three
1. It's described as a snare.
2. **Romans 8:31** Ultimately, it's only God's opinion that matters. And the Creator of the universe is *for us*.

Galatians 1:10 We have a choice. We can either seek to please people or seek to please God. We can't have it both ways.

Colossians 3:23 Whatever we do, our motive for doing it should be to please God, not to try to meet the expectations of people around us.
3. Answers will vary.

Lesson 2, Day Four
1. **John 10:10** It's described as an abundant life.

   1 Timothy 6:17 It's described as a life in which all the things God has provided for us are for our enjoyment.

   Isaiah 30:18 It's described as a life in which the Lord is waiting to be gracious to us, to show us mercy.
2. Answers will vary.
3. Answers will vary.

Lesson 3, Day One
1. Answers will vary.
2. **A.** It says that sin is not to have any power over me.
   B. We are under grace.
3. The law of the Spirit of life has set us free from the law of sin and death.

Lesson 3, Day Two
1. Our weapons are described as "not of flesh," as "enormously powerful," and as "capable of destroying fortresses."
2. The weapons of our battle are capable of destroying fortresses, arguments, and every pretension raising itself against the knowledge of God.
3. Answers will vary.
4. Answers will vary.

Lesson 3, Day Three
1. **A.** Our loins are girded in truth, righteousness is our breastplate, our feet are shod in readiness for the gospel of peace, faith is our shield, our salvation is our helmet, and the Word of God is our sword.
   B. Answers will vary.
2. Our second offensive weapon is prayer.
3. **A.** This is where it all begins. In baptism, we become adopted daughters of God with access to all the grace mentioned in this catechism passage: belief in, hope in, and love for God; the power to act as the Holy Spirit leads us; and the ability to grow in goodness through moral virtues.
   B. The Eucharist strengthens us to love heroically and to break disordered attachments to people and things that keep us from obeying God fully.
   C. When we take responsibility for our sins in the sacrament of penance, we are wielding a weapon that sends the devil running. We receive grace that will help us to resist sinning in the future.

Lesson 3, Day Four
1. We learn in 1 Corinthians 15:33 that bad company corrupts good character.
2. According to Colossians 3:1–10, we should be seeking things that are above and setting our minds on things that are above, not on things that are on earth. This is a description of the

things that will matter in the long run—in eternity. We're to put to death sexual immorality, impurity, passion, evil desire, and covetousness, which is idolatry, anger, wrath, malice, slander, obscene talk, and lies.
3. "The way of perfection passes by way of the Cross."

Lesson 4, Day One
1. **Isaiah 55:8–9** God's ways and thoughts are beyond us. We are not capable of understanding the mind of God or all His plans.
   Proverbs 3:5 We're told not to "lean on our own understanding" and to trust God instead.
2. Only at the end, when our partial knowledge ceases, when we see God face-to-face, will we understand His ways. This will only happen in heaven.
3. Answers will vary.
4. They are described as people who know God's name.

Lesson 4, Day Two
1. **Psalm 16:11** Abounding joy is found in God's presence. When He shows us the "path to life," we start to discover our purpose. That direction brings us joy.
   James 1:2 James says that joy comes through encountering trials—not because the trials are fun, but because they are worth it. They make our faith stronger as we learn to persevere.
   1 Peter 1:8–9 This passage says that indescribable and glorious joy comes when we "attain the goal of [our] faith," which is our eternal salvation.
2. Jesus focused on the joy that would come in the future if He obeyed in the present. His obedience was painful and costly, leading to the worst suffering imaginable. But the joy of knowing that His sacrifice would purchase our salvation helped Him obey His Father's will.
3. In this verse, Jesus was talking to the disciples, and acknowledging that they were in anguish. But He promised that He would return, and that no one would be able to take away their joy.

Lesson 4, Day Three
1. **A.** He disciplines the one He loves.
   B. He disciplines us for our benefit, so that we can grow in holiness.
   C. The peaceful fruit of righteousness will come to those who are disciplined and are trained by it.
2. Answers will vary.
3. Answers will vary.

Lesson 4, Day Four
1. Personal reflection.
2. Answers will vary.
3. **Psalm 100:5** God is good, merciful, and faithful. *Always.*
   Romans 8:31–32 God is *for us*. There is nothing He has held back from us that is for our good. He handed over His own Son *for us*.
   2 Peter 3:9 God is patient. He wants everyone to spend eternity with Him, and so He continues to intersect our lives with opportunities to let go of the things in the world that don't satisfy so we can fill our hearts with Him.

Lesson 5, Day One
1. Jesus addressed the parables to the Pharisees.
2. Jesus was welcoming sinners and eating with them.
3. Each of the parables in Luke 15 deals with something that has been lost and then found.

4. It's important to remember that the Pharisees spent all their time keeping the moral code. They didn't consider themselves the "one sinner who repents." They considered themselves one of "the righteous people." To hear that there would be more rejoicing over one sinner repenting than over their fastidious rule keeping likely offended them.

Lesson 5, Day Two
1. When the younger son asked for his inheritance while his father was still living, he showed great disrespect. It was as if he said, "I don't want you; I want your stuff. I'd be better off if you were dead. So why not just give me the money now?"
2. He was asking to be treated as one of the hired workers. He wasn't asking to be accepted as a son. He knew he didn't deserve that kind of treatment. But being hired as a worker would allow him to earn his keep.
3. When he was still a long way off, the father caught sight of him and began to run. Even before the son had a chance to offer his full apology, the father had asked that his best robe, sandals, and a ring be placed on his son. He asked that the fattened calf be slaughtered and a feast be prepared in his son's honor.
4. Answers will vary.

Lesson 5, Day Three
1. He was angry because he had stayed home, following the rules and working hard while his brother squandered his inheritance. His brother didn't deserve to be treated this way. The older son felt that if anyone had earned a party, he had. Instead of responding in anger, the older son might have expressed joy and relief that his brother was home.
2. The father came out and pleaded with him, inviting him to come in to the feast.
3. He said that all these years, he had served his father and never once disobeyed his orders, yet the father had never thrown a feast for him.

Lesson 5, Day Four
1. God will never give up on us. His patience will never wear thin. He seeks us out and calls us home.
2. The only reason God forgives us is out of "His sheer gratuitous love" (CCC 218). God's love for us is stronger than a mother's love for her children. It is the highest possible degree of love. God's love will be victorious over even the worst infidelities. He loves us so much that He gave what was most precious to Him, His Son, so that we could be forgiven (CCC 219). God's love is everlasting and steadfast (CCC 220).
3. Answers will vary.

Lesson 6, Day One
1. Psalm 90:14 says, "Fill us at daybreak with your mercy that all our days we may sing for you." Beginning the day with time alone with God sets the tone for the whole day. It resets our minds and reorients our priorities to better reflect what He wants for us. Even Jesus rose before it was light out in order to spend time alone with His Father.
2. Answers will vary.
3. Why wouldn't we welcome the input of the author of the Bible? One of the Holy Spirit's primary roles today is to guide us to truth. He takes the words of our heavenly Father and makes them known (and understandable) to us.

Lesson 6, Day Two
1. Answers will vary.
2. Answers will vary.
3. Answers will vary.
4. Answers will vary.
5. Answers will vary.
6. Answers will vary.
7. Answers will vary.

Lesson 6, Day Three
1. If we listen to God's words and act on them, we're like a wise man who builds his house on the rock. We'll have a foundation to stand on. No matter what hits us, we'll have something firm to cling to. But if we listen to those same words and don't act on them, we'll be standing on shifting sand. When crisis comes, we'll be vulnerable.
2. If we know the good we should do (after all, we just read about it), but fail to do it, we are in sin.
3. "Knowledge inflates with pride, but love builds up." When we build up a store of biblical knowledge, we can become prideful. The best antidote to this is to keep living out what we've read, growing more and more sacrificial in our love.

Lesson 6, Day Four
1. Answers will vary.
2. Answers will vary.
3. Answers will vary.

Prayer Pages

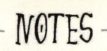# NOTES

walking with purpose

Dear God,

Thank you for being at work in me, giving me the desire and the power to do what pleases You.[27] I'm grateful for Your guidance, and that I can trust that Your plans for me are for my good and not for harm, to give me a future and a hope.[28] Please show me the way of life—the right choices to make—so that I have the joy of being in Your presence and the pleasure of living with You forever.[29] The enemy of my soul wants to steal, kill and destroy everything good in my life. But Your purpose and plan is to give me a rich and satisfying life of abundance.[30] Help me to remember that even when my circumstances are hard, You are always at work, causing everything to come together for my good.[31] May I see myself as Your masterpiece—Your beloved daughter—created anew in Christ so that I can do the good things You planned for me long ago.[32] To You be the glory—You who are able, through Your mighty power at work in me, to accomplish infinitely more than I can ask or imagine.[33]

Amen.

---

[27] Philippians 2:13
[28] Jeremiah 29:11
[29] Psalm 16:11
[30] John 10:10
[31] Romans 8:28
[32] Ephesians 2:10
[33] Ephesians 3:20

Opening Your Heart Series, Part III

Prayer Requests

Date:

Date:

Prayer Requests

Date:

Date:

Opening Your Heart Series, Part III

Prayer Requests

Date:

Date:

Prayer Requests

Date:

Date:

Prayer Requests

Date:

Donation Information

Walking with Purpose expands when women in parishes respond to the inspiration of the Holy Spirit and step forward to serve their neighbors and friends through this ministry. As the ministry grows, so do the material needs of the Walking with Purpose organization. If you would like to contribute to Walking with Purpose, donations can be mailed to:

Walking with Purpose
15 E. Putnam Avenue
Greenwich, CT 06830

You can also donate online at www.walkingwithpurpose.com. Walking with Purpose is a 501(c)(3) nonprofit organization. Your gift is fully tax deductible.

"See to it that no one misses the grace of God" Hebrews 12:15

It's time to stop talking about how there's nothing relevant out there for Catholic women.

IT'S TIME TO BE THE CHANGE WE WANT TO SEE.

You can bring **Walking with Purpose** to your parish!

IT'S EASY TO DO!

- **You've already got the skills needed!**
    - Personal commitment to Christ
    - Desire to share the love of Christ
    - Belief in the power of authentic, transparent community

- **We'll be there every step of the way, offering:**
    - Training
    - Mentoring
    - Bible study materials
    - Promotional materials

- **Do you think you have too many limitations to serve in this way?**

    Great! That's *exactly* where God wants us to start. If we will just offer Him *what we have*, He promises to do the rest. Few things stretch and grow our faith like stepping out and asking God to work through us. Say *YES*, and get ready to watch what He can do through imperfect women who depend on Him.

Learn more about bringing **Walking with Purpose** to your parish!

Visit us at **walkingwithpurpose.com**

walking with purpose

NOTES

"For to the one who has, more will be given"
Matthew 13:12

THANK YOU

for sharing this journey with all of us at **Walking with Purpose**.
We'd love to stay connected!
We've got more encouragement and hope available for you!

FREE valuable resources:

- Print out or download WWP Scripture Verses, can also be used as lock screens for phones.

- Join our community on Facebook, Twitter, Pinterest and Instagram for a daily boost!

- Subscribe to our Blog for regular inspiration and participate in conversations by contributing your comments!

The Walking with Purpose Bible study program is just the beginning.

Go to **walkingwithpurpose.com** to subscribe to our Blog and connect with us on Social Media

walking with purpose

NOTES

Walking with Purpose™ Young Adult Bible Studies

THE OPENING YOUR HEART SERIES

Beloved: *Opening Your Heart, Part I,* is a six-lesson Bible study that lays a strong foundation for our true identity as beloved daughters of God.

Unshaken: *Opening Your Heart, Part II,* is a six-lesson Bible study that fills our spiritual toolbox with exactly what we need to grow stronger in our faith.

Steadfast: *Opening Your Heart, Part III,* a six-lesson Bible study, unpacks why we are hustling for our worth and how to conquer our fears.

THE KEEPING IN BALANCE SERIES

Harmony: Keeping in Balance, Part I
Perspective: Keeping in Balance, Part II
Exhale: Keeping in Balance, Part III

THE DISCOVERING OUR DIGNITY SERIES

Tapestry: Discovering Our Dignity, Part I
Legacy: Discovering our Dignity, Part II
Heritage: Discovering Our Dignity, Part III

For more information on all Walking with Purpose Bible studies please visit us at
walkingwithpurpose.com

NOTES

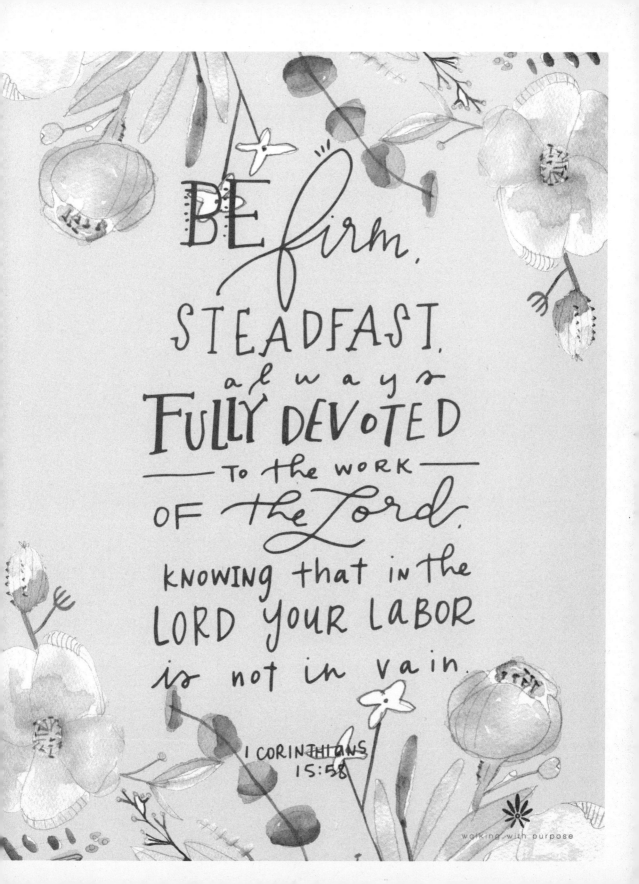

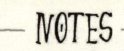
NOTES